THE POWER OF SELF-DISCIPLINE

SUSHMITA DUTTA

TRUE SIGN
PUBLISHING HOUSE

Published by True Sign Publishing House
Address: SY. No. 21/2 & 21/3, Sonnenahalli,
Krishnarajapura, Bengaluru,
Karnataka - 560049 India
E-mail: truesignbooks@gmail.com
Website: www.truesign.in

The Power Of Self-discipline

Author: Sushmita Dutta

ISBN:978-93-5805-909-0

First Edition: 2023

CONTENTS

Introduction

Self-discipline is the ability to control yourself and to work hard without needing anyone else to tell you what to do. It is an invaluable skill which helps us to learn and develop over the course of our life.

Self discipline means regulating oneself and making corrections to one's thoughts and behaviors in order to improve oneself. For students, this can mean: keeping yourself focused on assignments and in classes and not getting yourself distracted during lectures and making sure that you're on track with deadlines. This is especially important once you enter college, where you will need to rely on yourself in order to meet your academic goals.

Self-discipline is what makes the world go round. It teaches you self-control and how to shed bad habits. It's the ingredient that is necessary to stay persistent and resilient to accomplish your goals.

Examples of Self-Discipline

Self-discipline is like a muscle—the more you exercise it, the stronger it gets. And the stronger it gets, the easier it becomes to make better choices and maintain self control, especially when it matters.

In order to help you build self-discipline, get rid of bad habits that are preventing you from performing your best.

Given below are 10 self-discipline examples to practice and incorporate into your life:

1. Give yourself fewer decisions

People think of will-power as an all-or-nothing thing—we either have it or we don't. But will-power is best thought of as a tank that can fill and empty throughout the day and can be influenced by our choices and environment.

You can say 'no' to the temptation once and then say 'no' to it again later in the day. But till evening, that will-power muscle is worn out. So you arrive home after a long hard day and think, "Well, I've been so good. I deserve it," and you finally succumb to temptation.

In order to help you reduce decision fatigue, you can plan your to-lists and schedule in advance on a digital planner. Planning and seeing your priorities can help you mentally prepare for your tasks, manage time better, and, most importantly, stick to your scheduled tasks.

2. The 40% rule

The 40% rule is a principle that can help you push through when things get tough and a faster way to get around self-limiting beliefs.

When you're beginning to feel tired mentally and physically, you may feel like giving up, but in truth, you are only at forty per cent of what you are truly capable of achieving.

As a result, you may feel physically exhausted or mentally worn out when you are not really in any danger. In fact, you may still have 60% more effort to give! You are capable of much more than you think you are. Even when you genuinely feel too tired to carry on, you can recognize that this is just an excuse—you are not done; you are only forty per cent done.

3. The 10-minute rule 1.0

We overthink decisions with somewhat obvious answers, and we can rationalize bad behavior that robs us of more desirable outcomes. We're not always sure what's a real reason for hesitation and what's just a justification or excuse. That's where the 10-minute rule comes in.

4. The 10-minute rule 2.0

The 10-minute rule is both a productivity trick and a way to push through procrastination. This strategy will help you stay focused and improve your efficiency.

5. The 70% rule

The 70% rule is a great trick to help you shift your mindset and help you act even when you're feeling uncertain, scared or unwilling.

This rule was created by Jeff Bezos, who used it to help him achieve "escape velocity" out of a state of fear and get on the path of making choices, receiving feedback and adjusting along the way.

6. How to surf the urge?

An urge is simply a feeling of intense desire for something. You can intensely desire something good for you or something that has purely negative effects on you.

Does this mean ignoring the urge or temptation? Not quite. This is because when you try to ignore something, you may give it more psychological power and even prolong a sensation that would not have lasted that long. If we can do this for long enough, the urge does pass, and we are once again calm and balanced.

7. Change your relationship with discomfort

As a self-determining human being, you know that there is some room for negotiation. In order to grow, you must feel some pain and fear sometimes.

Nobody made sweeping life changes or achieved goals without breaking a sweat . It's hard. If it weren't hard, then everyone would be super successful, wouldn't they?

8. Action creates momentum

Whatever your goals are, motivation plays an important role and is one of the most important ingredients influencing your drive and ambition.

When we think about motivation, we look for something to light a spark in us and make us jump up from the couch and dive deeply into our tasks. We want motivation that causes action.

There are a few problems with this. This type of motivation, if you ever find it, is highly unreliable. If you feel you need motivation that causes action, you're doing it wrong.

For instance, a writer who feels they are unable to write without some form of motivation is going to stare at a blank page for hours.

The truth is, you should plan for life without a motivating kick start. Seeking that motivation creates a prerequisite to action. Get into the habit of proceeding without it. And surprisingly, this is where you'll find what you were seeking—action leads to motivation, more motivation, and eventually momentum.

9. Being organized

If you're already organized, you actually don't need as much self-discipline to get through your to-do list. You're already partway there. Instead of running around wondering if you have everything for the day, pack your bag the night before. Put your gym bag near the door, so you can't forget it and you don't have an excuse not to go.

Think about the small things you can do to organize yourself . If you do this, you can use your self-discipline for the things you really need it for.

10. The 10-10-10 rule

No matter how well you visualize your future self or how skilled you become at delaying gratification, you'll still inevitably face temptations that can overwhelm you.

If that means that you're about to lose your will-power and relapse into a harmful addiction from your past, you'll want to have a tool up your sleeve to help you stay disciplined.

Chapter 1

Importance of Self-Discipline

Have you heard about Fauja Singh, a Punjabi Sikh, who ran a marathon at the age of 100 years? He created history by breaking several world records in different age brackets and is a global inspiration today. People like Singh are examples of self-discipline. They are persistent and continue to chase their dreams irrespective of the challenges.

What is the meaning of Self-Discipline?

There are certain qualities that help people achieve success and happiness, but there's only one that leads to long-term achievement: self-discipline. Many of us expect instant gratification, which stops us from seeing the bigger picture. Self-discipline is that quality that enables us to pursue long-term goals, lead a healthy lifestyle and define happiness on our terms.

Contrary to popular belief, self-discipline isn't about being harsh or restricting ourselves from enjoying things. The true meaning of self-discipline is identifying one's goals and prioritizing them. Self-discipline helps one develop self-control, which is a sign of inner strength. It enables you to be consistent and stick to your decisions.

Need for Self-Discipline in life

Studies show that people with higher self-control are better equipped to avoid behaviors that may hamper their progress. In other words, they are not very affected by impulsive ideas or emotions. There is a need for discipline in life because it helps people do the following:

1. Build inner strength, character and stability
2. Resist unnecessary or harmful temptations
3. Improve chances of succeeding in what one chooses to do
4. Make rational decisions instead of impulsive ones
5. Practice patience, tolerance and persistence

Importance of Self-Discipline

There are several benefits of self-discipline. One of the biggest advantages of discipline is that it enables you to excel in professional settings. A disciplined person is focused, clear, productive and motivated at the workplace.

Let's look at some of the benefits of self-discipline at the workplace:

Helps Advance Your Career

When you persistently work towards fulfilling your targets, you stay on track with your work goals. Your managers are likely to notice your professionalism and may ask you to shoulder more responsibilities. This helps you grow in your career.

Lowers Stress Levels

Self-discipline helps you stay on track and monitor your work. When you meet deadlines and prioritize your objectives, you will stop worrying about chasing targets. This will help lower your anxiety and stress levels as you will have better control over your life.

Boosts Self-Confidence

The importance of self-discipline is reflected in the fact that it leads to improved self-esteem. When you're productive and achieve your goals regularly, it creates a sense of pride. You feel confident about your abilities and you find meaning and purpose in your work.

Enhances Professional Relationships

Practicing self-discipline helps you stay on top of your tasks and feel more motivated and positive. It encourages you to collaborate with others and solve problems efficiently. Your positive attitude will make others want to work with you.

How to develop Self-Discipline?

People aren't always born with self-discipline; most of us learn and develop it over time. When you know where you're headed, it's easier to stay focused on your goals.

Here are some simple yet effective ways to develop self-discipline:

Identify your strengths and weaknesses

Differentiate between the qualities you already possess and things that you'd like to improve. Knowing what needs improvement is key to bettering yourself. If you have trouble making this differentiation, you can always reach out to your friends or peers and get constructive feedback.

Define your expectations

An effective way to work towards self-improvement is to define your needs, expectations and goals. When you develop a plan, it helps you focus on your priorities. Remember to set realistic and achievable goals. Your dreams should be realistic.

Measure your progress

You need to monitor and track your progress to remain consistent in your work. When you create a plan to achieve your goals make sure you also decide how to measure your progress. You can set milestones by breaking tasks into smaller goals. This will help you understand how far you have come and how far you have to go.

Learn from the situation

There may be days when you are unable to meet your targets. Remember, it's perfectly normal to have setbacks! Accept the mistakes or setbacks and learn from them so you can avoid them in the future. Remember, self-discipline also includes managing negative emotions and picking oneself up when one stumbles. Always learn to forgive yourself.

Chapter 2

Benefits of Self-Discipline

Self-discipline is a quality which professionals use to attain sustainable success over time. Regardless of your role or industry, self-discipline can help you complete tasks efficiently. Learning about self-discipline's benefits and how to develop it can help improve your professional life and achieve career success.

Why explore the benefits of Self-Discipline?

Understanding the possible benefits of self-discipline and its importance is a practical step toward achieving your career goals. Professionals use many skills and qualities to attain career success, and self-discipline is an essential part of staying motivated to do so. This quality enables you to be patient with your decisions and plans until you accomplish them.

Self-discipline is a quality that enables you to discover your unique strengths . It fosters the ability to focus on goals to achieve a specific result. Self-disciplined professionals often use qualities, such as responsibility, drive, ambition, and motivation to excel at work. In the workplace, self-discipline promotes the mindset that allows you to perform duties efficiently, meet designated deadlines, and complete projects successfully.

Why is Self-Discipline important?

Self-discipline is important because it provides the opportunity to succeed professionally. It can aid your personal and professional development by helping you set a work routine and remain accountable for your goals. A significant characteristic of self-discipline is the ability to gain satisfying results after putting time and effort into performing tasks. Self-discipline enables you to make decisions and follow them. Maintaining self-discipline is essential to improving confidence, self-esteem, and intrinsic strength, facilitating a healthier and more productive life, both personally and professionally.

How to become more Self-Disciplined?

1. Identify areas of improvement

Consider the skills and qualities you wish to improve to foster better work performance. It may entail increasing your task efficiency, developing a better time management system, or organizing your assignments. Knowing the specific areas you want to improve can enable you to create and implement a plan to enhance your self-discipline. If you can't decide on the qualities requiring improvement, consider asking your colleagues for constructive feedback. This can help you better understand your strengths and improvement areas.

2. Determine your expectations and goals

After identifying the areas requiring improvement, you can set your expectations and goals accordingly. Consider creating a work plan to improve your qualities and job performance. For example, you can determine the priority of your tasks or create daily schedules to ensure you meet deadlines. Defining your expectations and setting achievable goals can help you build self-discipline.

3. Make an effort to achieve defined goals

Next, you can take steps to accomplish these goals. Consider visualizing the possible outcomes after completing each goal, such as a promotion, raise, or compliments from your manager. This can help motivate you further and encourage you to focus on your tasks. You can also motivate yourself by determining when you're most productive and planning to complete your important tasks during those periods.

4. Monitor your progress

Monitoring your progress is essential in building self-discipline and reaching specific goals. For example, suppose you're a content creator and aim to share more videos overall. You can create a goal to upload five videos every week. This allows you to evaluate your improvement and discipline yourself to meet that weekly target. Consider rewarding yourself with something you enjoy after reaching the milestones to increase your motivation and remain productive in the following weeks.

Benefits of Self-Discipline

Here are some significant benefits of self-discipline:

Makes you more productive

Self-discipline is an important feature that can help you become more productive. It allows you to focus on your strengths when completing projects or assignments. You can learn to perform duties faster to increase productivity or read documents effectively to understand information more accurately. Focusing on your strengths and improving them can facilitate better results that make you more productive.

Improves time management

The ability to manage your time efficiently is another benefit of self-discipline . Time management helps you discipline yourself, define your priorities and honour your commitments. With self-discipline, you can be deliberate about selecting a critical task to complete at a particular time and work solely on that task.

Increases your focus

Once you have self-discipline, you can remain focused on your tasks. Self-discipline helps you recognize the importance of the activity you intend to complete. It also makes you recognize the effort, time, and resources you're contributing to accomplishing that specific assignment. If you clearly understand your goals and your plans to achieve them, self-discipline can increase your focus and dedication to meeting those goals.

Helps you learn skills faster

Professionals with self-discipline usually have an inner drive to excel. Self-discipline helps you use that drive to gain additional skills, such as research, organization, or critical thinking, which can help improve how you execute work assignments. Your effort and commitment to learning these skills can make you learn them faster.

Makes you discover new talent

Self-discipline can prompt you to sign up for more career-related courses or certifications that introduce you to talents you may not consider previously. It's one reason working professionals prioritize self-discipline in the workplace. It helps you seek additional areas to explore to foster growth and add to your existing skill sets.

Reduces your anxiety and stress levels

Self-discipline allows you to follow your plans to achieve your personal and workplace goals. This prevents you from struggling at work or submitting tasks after the deadline. As a self-disciplined professional, you're more able to remain organized and meet deadlines on time. This can lower your anxiety and stress and help you feel more relaxed at work.

Helps you persevere

Self-discipline gives you the ability to continue with a task despite challenges. This skill helps you to resume working on a project even after your initial excitement disappears. Perseverance is essential to achieve any goal, and this usually requires discipline.

Improves your personal and workplace relationships

Focusing on tasks and goals can make you feel positive and motivated and extend that energy to others. The happiness and confidence you feel can impact the workplace positively and promote healthier work relationships. It can also help reach your friends and colleagues and motivate them to do the same and feel better about themselves. A self-disciplined professional can also gain the respect of colleagues at work, which can help sustain a good work reputation.

Increases your chances of career advancement

Self-discipline can make you envision your company's goals and create plans to contribute to them. If company management or your immediate supervisor notices your behaviours, actions, and impressive work performance, they can decide to offer a promotion or assign you more significant projects. This can help increase your chances of advancing to a higher position in the company.

Chapter 3

How to practise Self-Discipline successfully?

One can adopt the following ways to ensure you're maintaining self-discipline in the workplace:

Eliminate distractions

It can be easier to avoid distractions when you resist temptation. You can accomplish this by leaving social media platforms or keeping your phone aside until completing all the tasks. You can also create time slots to focus solely on specific tasks in your daily schedule. If you have colleagues who come to your space to socialize regularly, you can inform them about your program so that they don't distract you.

Take a break

Giving your brain rest from complicated tasks can allow you to focus on additional duties requiring your attention. Consider taking a short walk or browsing the internet with your phone for a few minutes. You can monitor the duration of the short breaks to discipline yourself. Try using your phone to set a timer for five to ten minutes while taking a break, and you can resume your work when it buzzes.

Practise self-care

Caring for your health can improve your focus and enable you to commit to assigned duties. You can maintain self-discipline by getting enough sleep every night, exercising, maintaining a healthy work-life balance, and having a nutritious diet. Consider taking the time to practise self-care to help you sustain and increase motivation for work.

Chapter 4

How to build Self-Discipline?

Self-discipline occurs in that part of the brain responsible for focus, impulse control, and emotion. That means that it's a psychological function connected to emotion and impulses.

That's why it's often in conflict with the logical, rational part of our brains. In order to change our behavior, we have to tap into neuroscience-backed strategies to change.

The more you change, the easier this becomes as your brain resets to connect reward centers to disciplined behavior. Follow these steps to start working toward a goal in your life.

1. Identify growth areas.

First, start by examining areas of your life that you'd like to improve. If you're not sure where to start, write down how you spend your time in a day. Look at your calendar or phone for clues. Then, reflect on what you value and ask yourself whether your behaviors uphold those values. Once you apply self-discipline in one area of your life, the skills will transfer to all other areas.

2. Choose your goal (and start small).

Now that you've identified some growth areas, choose one to focus on first. Start small by choosing an area that you believe is easiest to achieve. That way, you can experience the emotional rewards of success quickly, enabling you to move on to more ambitious goals.

3. Visualize your outcome.

Did you know that you're more likely to reach your goals if you write them down? The act of writing down goals creates a link in the physical world to what's going on in your head and serves as a reminder.

This can be as simple as a sticky note on your computer monitor or as complex as a vision board. Visualizing yourself achieving your goals can also give you a greater chance of success.

4. Set your environment.

Before you start, make changes to your environment to increase your chances of success. Some studies show that your environment makes a difference for people trying to achieve exercise goals.

If you want to read more, cancel Netflix or delete social media apps from your phone — whatever you know might distract you. Changing your environment also signals to you that something has changed.

5. Don't wait for it to feel right.

If you wait for your schedule to clear up, your kids to get older, or your inbox to reach a manageable level, you might never get started on the work that needs to be done. Embrace every moment and try to do your best work.

6. Know how you'll measure progress.

If you don't know how you'll measure progress, it will be difficult to know whether you're succeeding. Be sure to set a goal that's measurable.

Instead of "be a better father," you may want to set a goal like "spend two hours of 1:1 time with my daughter each week." In a business , look at what goals you want to achieve and then work backward to see what activities it'll take to get there. If you want to reach your sales quota for one month, start by identifying how many meetings you should book and set a goal for yourself for each week.

7. Get an accountability partner.

Asking for accountability, particularly from someone you live with, can go a long way to build self-discipline. You can engage in one-way accountability, where you ask someone to check in with you or hold you accountable at regular intervals. The best kind of accountability, though, is two-way accountability where two people commit to hold each other accountable for a set period.

The social pressure of knowing someone will ask you about how you're doing is a powerful motivator and doesn't take the self away from self-discipline.

8. Lighten your load.

Dr. Abby Medcalf explains that will-power is an exhaustible resource. You may have full motivation at the start of the day, but by the time you hit 6 p.m., your self-control has been broken away.

Your car broke down, you burned dinner, and now your boss just texted asking you to work on something tonight. At this point, you just throw in the towel and pour yourself a glass of whatever you're trying to avoid.

Set yourself up for success by taking things off your plate. Get that cleaning service to give yourself more free time, or simply say no to some commitments you can live without.

9. Build new reward associations.

It feels safe to follow patterns we know, and we've established reward associations — for instance, the delicious taste of eating a huge bowl of ice cream.

In one study of app-based mindfulness training, participants used a craving tool to report their responses to eating different foods and amounts. After using the tool just 10 times in some cases, participants reduced their craving-based behavior by 40% just by being aware of how they felt.

By paying close attention to how you feel when you perform an old or new action, you can re-evaluate your old reward loops.

10. Fail.

It's not that those with self-discipline never have days where they spend 45 minutes on social media, and lose two prospects — all before 10:00 AM.

They definitely have these days, but then they wake up the next morning and start over.

Self-discipline is the act of trying, failing, and trying again. Know what your plan is when you fail. Check in with your partner, and be ready to try again the next day.

11. Take care of yourself.

Self-discipline is worth very little if you're hurting yourself to achieve it. Chasing some goals can come at the expense of your overall health and create new problems.

If you're burning the midnight oil for weeks or months on end to be more "self-disciplined," you've missed the point.

Part of self-discipline is taking care of yourself. Breaks throughout the day, a healthy diet, time in nature, and healthy relationships will recharge you to help you stay focused on your goal. As Dr. Abby Medcalf says, your day starts when you choose to go to bed and set your alarm the night before.

12. Use time blocking.

If your biggest excuse for change is that you're too busy, there's a way to play yourself at your own game. Time blocking is a method of scheduling time on your calendar not just for meetings, but for rest, focus time, and dreaded activities you just keep putting off.

Alongside meetings, there's time blocked for workouts, focus time, end-of-day admin tasks, and lunch. For a busy executive (or any other person), this ensures that the most urgent tasks don't nudge out important tasks that need focus time.

At first glance, this may look like there's no white space in your schedule at all. Time blocking doesn't mean that every hour is busy, it just means that every hour is intentional.

13. Treat youeself.

Too much deprivation often means we start justifying bad behaviors. This often sounds like, "I've earned this," or "I deserve this." This is often the beginning of the end of our progress. Instead, give yourself treats throughout your self-discipline practice. These treats, whether a nice dinner or a new pair of shoes, will help you feel restored and balanced.

14. Forgive yourself.

You must forgive yourself when you slip. What's important is that you move forward. To do that you've got to forgive yourself.

Give yourself some grace. Did you fail to meet your goal? Will you have to work hard tomorrow to catch up? Will this have any effect on your long-term progress?

Once you've looked at the impact of your slip, you can decide how to move forward and get back on track.

15. Set bigger goals.

Once you achieve a small goal, you'll feel a sense of reward. You can set a bigger goal and use the same strategies to continue or tackle a different area of your life.

Remember, self-discipline is a practice. You will not be perfect every day. What's important is showing up each day ready to try. So, what changes are you going to make today?

Chapter 5

How to Discipline yourself?

"Once you have commitment, you need the discipline and hard work to get you there." — Haile Gebrselassie

In the heart of any successful person, lies self-discipline. Whether it's success in their personal lives or their professional lives, it all starts with an inherent ability for self-control through discipline. Your thoughts, emotions, behaviors and your habits. You must keep them all in check.

If you want to achieve those lofty goals you set, understanding how to discipline yourself is a key ingredient to the success story. But self-discipline isn't something new. In fact, self-discipline has been a topic of discussion for thousands of years. And it's been championed by some of the world's most successful people.

Referring to our ability to succeed in life at any endeavor, **Aristotle** once said, "Good habits formed at youth make all the difference." We can't form those good habits without having a handle on our ability to discipline our actions and behaviors.

Theodore Roosevelt once said, "With self-discipline most anything is possible." More recently, **Jim Rohn** claimed "Discipline is the bridge between goals and accomplishment." And **Robert Kiyosaki** asserted that "Confidence comes from discipline and training." What successful people have come to understand is that discipline is the gateway to the achievement of their goals. They learned how to use discipline in their lives to achieve their dreams. They leveraged the art of self-discipline by creating a foundational set of good habits that helped them to see things through.

And so can you.

But how is discipline created or formed? What allows one person to wield what seems like total and full control over their behaviors and their actions, while others falter and fail? How can one person be so conscious of what they do on a daily basis, while others simply throw caution to the wind?

The answer to those questions lies in our habits. Since 40% of our behavior is habit-driven, if you want to control your ability to be self-disciplined, you have to control your habits.

There are 10 habits that will help you to discipline yourself. If you can instill these 10 habits into your life, you can create the foundation for achieving your goals. Without these habits, you'll just be stabbing around in the dark.

Habits: The road to Self-Discipline

Considering that what we do on a daily basis is habit-driven, developing the right habits will help to instill the right amount of discipline into our lives.

But where do habits come from and how are they developed? And why is that when we try to change our habits by either breaking bad habits or building good habits, we only follow through for so long before we give up and revert to our old ways?

The biggest problem, especially with habits that we've had for years and even decades, are the neural pathways that have been etched in our brains. Neural pathways help to link up neural networks to perform a particular function such as walking up the stairs, smoking a cigarette, or preparing a cup of coffee in a certain way.

Neural pathways help to automate behavior that's constantly repeated in an effort to reduce conscious-processing power in the mind. This allows the mind to focus on other things that might be going on. This stems from our early days as humans, and is part of our genetic makeup, allowing for a more efficient mind that can be used towards many other things rather than the mundane.

However, it's the supposed mundane behaviors that are repeated, which work to hold us back in most cases. We tend to have more bad habits that are detrimental to our lives than good habits that help to move us forward. Considering that those neural pathways get etched deeper and deeper over time, it becomes harder and harder to break bad habits or make even to form good ones when the bad ones get in the way.

But, if you can instill the following habits into your life, you'll find that disciplining yourself becomes far easier. It won't happen overnight. Remember that habits take time to form and to break. But, if you start small, and build, you won't be wondering how you can discipline yourself any longer, since you'll embody the particular habits that promote self discipline in life.

1. Gratitude

The habit of gratitude helps move us away from constantly wanting what we don't have, and towards appreciating what we do have. When we do this, some remarkable shifts begin to occur.

The effects of gratitude are far-reaching. From improving our mental health, to our emotional well-being, and our spirituality, gratitude can do so much. But most importantly, it helps to move us away from a state of lack and towards a state of abundance.

When we live in a state of lack, it becomes downright impossible to focus on being disciplined and achieving our goals. We spend so much of our mental capacity on worrying about what we don't have and living in a state of fear, that we forget about what we do have.

The state of lack translates into physical ailments. It produces stress and releases stress hormones , which impacts a number of systems in our body. When we stress, our digestive, reproductive, and immune systems are all adversely affected.

Spend 10 minutes every day writing out all the things that you're grateful for. Even if you feel you have nothing to be grateful for, find something.

2. Forgiveness

When we spend a large portion of our days in a state of anger, regret or guilt, we create more problems . Hate and anger consumes far more energy than love and forgiveness. When we forgive, we learn to let go of certain things.

Without the habit of forgiveness, we couldn't achieve self-discipline. We're too worried about how someone wronged us to even focus on discipline or achieving our goals.

If someone hurt you, learn to forgive them. It doesn't necessarily mean you have to forget. Just forgive and release that negative energy back into the universe.

By forgiving, we let go of negativity. If you want to learn how to discipline yourself, forgiveness is surely one main avenue. Think about all the people that you're angry with or that have wronged you, and write down why you forgive them. Try to put yourself in their shoes. What would you have done in their situation? Try to find some solution.

3. Meditation

Meditation helps to put our minds at ease. When we meditate, we miss out all the noise and realize that we're just one of many beings in this universe.

Meditation also has a big impact on our ability to be self-disciplined. It helps to improve our mental, emotional, physical, and spiritual health all at once, allowing you to reap some of the biggest results for minimal time invested.

Meditation doesn't take long. It can be done in 10 or 15 minutes. Keep your mind still and don't let it wander. When it starts to wander, bring it back. Feel your energy grounded in the earth, open your palms to face the heavens, and really feel the air as it moves in and out of your lungs.

Meditation is about aligning our physical bodies with our spiritual bodies. When we can align the two, we can live a more focused life by not worrying about the common things that tend to weigh us down. It helps to lighten our load.

4. Active Goal Setting

Active goals have a profound meaning. They're specific and measurable. And you have a plan towards their attainment. When we set long-term goals in this manner, and we also engage in active goal setting on a daily basis, it's far easier to achieve our dreams.

Active goal setting instills discipline because it gives us direction. It also helps us to avoid distractions by seeing just what needs to be done in a given day. Without active goals, we're left like a ship without a sail stuck in stormy waters.

To set active goals, first you must set some long-term goals. If you have long-term goals, then you need to engage in monthly, weekly, and daily goal setting and planning. And you also have to actively track your progress towards your goals.

5. Eat Healthy

Raw foods and fruits offer the biggest boost for energy because they require less energy to process and provide more energy . The amount of energy we have plays a large role in how focused we are. When we're focused, we can approach our goals with discipline.

It's important to not only eat a healthy breakfast, but to eat healthy throughout the day. To do this, you have to plan your meals and break some bad habits. If you eat fast food every day, you're not going to have the energy to approach your goals with enthusiasm or have the discipline to follow through.

Food has a large influence on the mind-body connection. Opt for raw, healthy, and organic foods when you can and limit your intake of junk.

6. Sleep

Sleep is directly connected with our ability to discipline ourselves. When we don't get enough sleep, it affects our mood, ability to focus, our judgement, our diet, and our overall health.

Studies indicate that people who are deprived of the proper amount of sleep on a regular basis are at a greater risk for certain diseases. The lack of sleep has a great impact on our immune system.

It's important to get at least 6 hours of sleep, no matter what. Stay away from too many toxins throughout the day such as alcohol, cigarettes, or prescription medicine, if it can be avoided.

Overall, the benefits of getting enough sleep are far-reaching. Aside from helping you to be more disciplined, it will improve your memory, curb inflammation and pain, lower stress, spur your creativity, sharpen your attention, help you avoid depression, and limit your chances for accidents.

7. Exercise

Exercise acts as a cornerstone to a life filled with good and positive habits and free from bad habits.

While many people are busy running around, trying to get things done in the day, they're failing to take the bull by the horn when they don't exercise. Many people think that they can't build up this habit or they have too much to do to worry about, rather than exercising.

By instilling the habit of exercise, not only can you become more disciplined, but you can improve your life in a number of ways. First, exercise reduces your levels of stress and pain by releasing endorphins such as dopamine and serotonin.

Second, exercise improves health by increasing blood flow and oxygenation of the body's cells, helping to fight off diseases and boost the immune system. And, of course, exercise increases our ability to focus on the task at hand, allowing us to lead a more disciplined life.

To instill the habit of exercise in your life, start by walking around the block for 5 minutes in the morning. Just 5 minutes. Do that for one week. Then, increase it to 10 minutes and do that for a week. And continue with this pattern. Eventually, exercise will become a full-blown habit.

8. Organization

To be self-disciplined and achieve our goals, we need to be organized. Organization is a habit that needs to be wholly embodied, not only in your professional life, but also in your personal life. This includes organizing the items in your home and office along with the items in your mind.

An organized life is a disciplined life. For example, start by organizing your desk drawer. The next day, move onto organizing your medicine cabinet in your bathroom. And so on. Do one small thing a day to improve your organization. That's all it takes.

It's the little things that we do on a daily basis that have a large impact on the quality of our lives. Pay attention to the small stuff and you'll reap large benefits.

9. Time Management

When we can properly manage our time, we have room for activities that will help us achieve our goals. In order to achieve our long-term goals, we have to perform actions that might not be urgent, but are most certainly important.

However, our ability for self-discipline is largely derived from our ability to effectively manage our time. The prominent time managers of the world are also some of the most successful people in their respective fields. Why? Because they use time as a benefit rather than a detractor.

10. Persistence

Persistence is that habit that helps us to not give up. Even when we do fail, it allows us to get back up again. Without the habit of persistence, self-discipline would be largely impossible.

Why? Because achieving our goals is hard. Getting discouraged is easy. And giving up takes far less effort than continuing to push through, especially towards something that inflicts a lot of pain before it provides us with any pleasure.

What we need to do is realize that even the most famous people who succeeded in life have failed many times over. Failure is an important stepping-stone in life. Without failing, and failing big, we couldn't achieve the lofty goals that we set for ourselves.

There are certainly many ways to instill this habit, but the best way is to really come up with some profound reasons as to why you want the things in life that you do. When our reasons are strong enough, they can get us through just about anything.

Chapter 6

Types of Self-Discipline

There are many ways that we can implement self-discipline everyday. Here are examples of three types: active discipline, reactive discipline and proactive discipline.

Active discipline is doing what you need to in that very moment such as eating a healthy meal, limiting your distractions while studying, and exercising.

You were actively disciplined when you chose to eat healthy instead of unhealthy. You were disciplined when you took the time to study and turned your phone off. Another example is when you decided to exercise instead of watch TV or surf the internet.

Reactive discipline is controlling your thoughts or behaviors when dealing with unforeseen situations such as getting a flat tire on your way to work, dealing with a rude person, and locking your car keys in your car.

Instead of complaining, you used these situations as opportunities to learn. When you got the flat tire, you got the tire fixed. In that moment, you chose to be grateful that it was just a flat tire and no one was hurt.

When dealing with that rude person, you realized that their rudeness was their issue and not yours. You understood that "an eye for an eye" leaves everyone blind. You decided to treat that person with extra kindness because they needed it.

You locked your car keys in the car. You said to yourself, "It's okay, mistakes happen." You realize the importance of forgiving yourself and moving on. You know that this is just one minor setback during your full 24 hour day.

Proactive discipline is doing things in advance in an effort to better control a situation such as bringing an umbrella on a rainy day, creating a to-do list, and going to bed on time.

You watched the news that morning and prepared for the weather. You had goals that you needed to accomplish on a deadline and decided to create a to-do list to prioritize those goals. Instead of staying up late, you decided to go to bed early to wake up on time the next day.

Admittedly, it is hard to commit to self-discipline everyday. Self-discipline is no easy feat because we are constantly faced with issues that seem to occur at the most bothersome time.

It is true that we have no control over what can happen but we do have control over how we react to what happens. We also have access and opportunity to practice techniques that enable us to exercise self-discipline and reach our vision.

Practicing Self-Discipline

Lack of self-discipline delays us from accomplishing our vision and failure to implement self-discipline techniques causes us to stray away from our vision.

When determining self-discipline techniques, consider your vision statement and these six questions.

- What can you do in this very moment to achieve what you want to accomplish?
- If you encounter a set back, how will you react to it?
- What is the worst thing that can happen or what might go wrong?
- Do you have a method to deal with it?
- How can you prepare to achieve your vision?

- What should you begin doing today that can help you reach your vision tomorrow?

Now, remember how that exercise made you feel? Good! I'll share a **secret** that I've used for sometime to help with self-discipline and accomplishing my vision.

Practicing self-discipline and achieving your vision happens when three things occur:

1. You feel good while achieving your vision,
2. You do not allow set-backs to control your feelings, and
3. You feel good after your vision is accomplished.

Chapter 7

How does Self-Discipline impact students' life?

Self-discipline is an excellent trait to master when you are a student as you are continuously adding & deleting things from your life.

Discipline plays a colossal part in deciding the course of your life and significantly impacts your thoughts and actions. Not everyone is equipped with the amount of self-discipline that is required of them. It is almost the foundational basis for any long-term goal that has to be accomplished through hard work and perseverance. Self-discipline is commonly defined as conducting yourself rationally, without your emotions infiltrating your thoughts. In simple words, the behavior where you do not lose self-control and get carried away.

What is self-discipline for students and how shall they practice it?

Self-discipline is a very important habit for students of all ages but especially those belonging to school and college because these are the formative years when you learn as many new skills as possible and try to expand the horizon of your knowledge.

As a student, completing your homework and assignments daily, revising everyday lessons, reaching school or college on time, being attentive in class, attending all lectures, doing the follow-up with teachers and professors, meeting deadlines, managing your time, and reserving some of it for extra-curricular are some acts that you can engage in, to be self-disciplined. This applies more to college students because this is the period when you start learning to be independent and have to take up a lot of responsibility on your shoulders at the same time as being exposed to the world. Thus, it requires a lot of discipline to finish your work on time as well as balance other aspects of life.

Importance of Self-Discipline for students

Many of you might wonder why discipline is emphasized over and over again. After all, what is so great about being able to practice it in the right way, that too when you are a student. Well, these are some of the greatest benefits of leading a disciplined life as a student:

It improves your academic performance

As **Swami Vivekananda** rightly observed, " Education is the manifestation of perfection" every student needs a lot of discipline to strive for this perfection and the journey is ever so much important than the destination. You just can't expect to rank in class after spending a rather idyllic year and mugging up everything right before 20 days of your exam. No, that's very taxing on your mental health would never yield desirable results. We all know that success is never served on a platter; either you work for it or let go of it. There's no convenient middle ground between the two. And successful students require to study round the year with a fair balance of healthy meals, sufficient sleep, and enough energy so that they can come out with flying colors.

Key to a stress-free life

Maintaining a disciplined life will enable you to complete your projects and home works on time and thus save you the stress of last-minute rushes because you begged them to allow a delayed submission.

Multiplies your self-confidence

Brian Tracy said, " Every act of self-discipline increases your confidence, trust, and belief in yourself and your abilities" and it's indisputably true. Working on yourself and self-discipline would mean improvement and as you get better day-by-day, your confidence grows in leaps and bounds. You become more sure of yourself and your abilities, and in the process, people around you also start deeming you as a responsible student and entrust you with more responsibilities. Your teachers also start relying on you.

Helps in time management

Having completed your work much ahead of time, you will have a lot of time for other activities that you are involved in. For example, if you finish your term papers on time and submit them, you will have a lot of time at hand for administering the activities of a society in college that you head or go back home early and get back to painting if that's your hobby or watch a movie with at the weekend with friends.

Uplifts your reputation

It would not be foolish to say that self-discipline becomes your identity as a student after a point in time. You become known for your punctuality, constant efforts, and responsible nature in your friend circle and the neighbourhood. More and more people respect you as a result of this and you enjoy the benefits of an untainted reputation throughout your student life, which is a great perk, after all.

Enables you to shrug off temptations in a jiffy

You cannot allow yourself to dissociate while you are studying or doing some other work and self-discipline helps you restrict that. There will always be a phone buzzing or a party invitation waiting but once you've set your goal and made up your mind to achieve it at any cost, you won't succumb to these temporary amusements because you know where to reach.

Example of Self-Discipline for Students

Know your limits

As much as it is important to make friends and socialize, it is equally important to know when and where to draw the line. Prioritizing friends and night-outs over assignments can be harmful to your academic growth. Go out, have fun, play, enjoy but keep a specific part of the day for doing this, and do not kill up all your study time for friends or family. That would hamper your discipline in more ways than you can think of.

Reward yourself frequently

The human mind functions on motivation. So, you should always remember to reward yourself with breaks at regular intervals after fulfilling a goal or a good ice cream treat which will keep you undeterred on your path to pursue self-discipline. You will have a sense of being disciplined and yet, you won't be stressing yourself too much.

Work hard but smart

Of course it is not at all easy to be a disciplined student and demands a lot of patience and honest efforts, but you need to have a defined plan for every day. You list down your work and assign them different schedules throughout the day and not only that, try completing them within the stipulated time. That's how you reduce your workload and get done with your work with effortless elan.

Remove Distractions

Recognize your distractions well. Smartphones are potential distractions to students because they are not usually well-versed with self-restraint techniques, and thus you should consider abandoning your smartphone at least when you study. Switching to 'aeroplane mode' or switching it off may be a good idea to detach yourself temporarily.

Follow a routine

Well, this might sound like the school principal giving long, boring pieces of irritating advice at the morning assembly but it truly works wonders. If you are a student and you find yourself thoroughly indisciplined, check your weekly activities, commitments and make a routine today itself. Make a point to abide by it. This influences the process of building self-discipline in students and makes it a lot more easier

The most important part of self-discipline is consistency and a positive attitude. Naturally, you will keep getting distracted and lose patience but you cannot ever afford to get so discouraged that you ultimately give in to indisciplined behavior. Practising all of these methods over a considerable period, regularly is the only key to mastering the art of self-discipline your budding minds!

Chapter 8

Self-Control vs Self-Discipline

What is Self-Discipline?

Control over your conscious decisions to do or not do, say or not talk, think or imagine at any time is what self-discipline is. Self-discipline refers to the mind's ability to govern the body. Self-discipline is concerned with conscious judgments about conduct, whereas self-control is concerned with emotions and the things we do reflexively to defend our bodies and egos whenever they are under attack. Self discipline is a life-style.

What is Self-Control?

Self-control refers to the feelings, behaviors, and reactions that we have learned in this and previous incarnations and that occur automatically when the suitable stimulus is presented.

Self-control does not imply not having emotions, wants, or anxieties, or not being fully immersed in all that happens around you. It is about being in control of oneself regardless of your emotions, thoughts, or bodily sensations.

Self Control - saying 'no' to implulses

It is learning to remain unaffected by them in order to preserve balance, calm, and the capacity to think rationally during any perilous or emotionally intense encounter. Self-control entails exercising control over your reactions and interactions even when you have no control over the circumstance.

How are they different yet related?

The definitions of the two terms are nearly identical. However, psychologically, we can distinguish between the two processes. 'No or stop', says self-control. 'Go, and keep going', says self-discipline.

Self-control requires us to quit doing what we are already doing, sometimes in the middle of it. Self-discipline motivates us to begin and complete new work or endeavors. When we have a second chestnut in our hands, self-control prevents us from devouring it. Self-control prevents us from grabbing the second chestnut the following time. Habits are challenged by self-control. It opposes emotional comforts for the sake of enjoyment.

Self-discipline requires us to get up and get out of bed. We don't click the snooze button because we have self-control. We should do something even if we don't feel like it, according to self-discipline. Whereas irregular is more enjoyable, it demands regularity and forethought. It expects us to fulfill deadlines, produce something, and take responsibility.

How they affect our lives?

Self-control is in the moment, self-discipline is a way of life.

Self-sabotage can be avoiding exercising discipline due to a lack of self-control. Inconsistency and inconsistent implementation of the desired discipline might undermine our efforts at self-control due to a lack of self-discipline.

Self-control is more primitive than self-discipline. It frequently refers to eating, smoking, drinking, and other physical pleasures that provide momentary psychological consolation.

Self-discipline is a more advanced use, mainly refers to achievements, future plans, and dreams for wealth and success. It has to do with arriving to work on time and adhering to academic or workplace norms. Helps encourage us to forego some of our present pursuits in order to pursue more fulfilling ones later. Such as the practice of continuing to study throughout one's life. It has required us to work longer hours in order to enhance our status and boost our revenue. It recommends that we completely finance our retirement plan and avoid incurring credit card debt.

Chapter 9

How to Improve your Self-Control?

Self-control is the ability to regulate and alter your responses to avoid undesirable behaviors, increase desirable ones, and achieve long-term goals. Research has shown that possessing self-control can be important for health and well-being.

Psychologists define self-control as:

- The ability to control behaviors to avoid temptations and achieve goals
- The ability to delay gratification and resist unwanted behaviors or urges
- A limited resource that can be depleted

People use various terms for self-control, including discipline, determination, grit, willpower, and fortitude. Some researchers believe that self-control is partly determined by genetics, but it is also a skill you can strengthen with practice.

Self-control is one aspect of executive function, a set of abilities that helps people to plan, monitor, and achieve their goals. People with attention-deficit attention disorder (ADHD) often have characteristics linked to problems with executive function.

Types of Self-Control

There are three primary types of self-control:

Impulse control refers to the ability to manage urges and impulses. People who struggle with impulse control may act first without thinking about the consequences of their actions.

Emotional control refers to the ability to regulate emotional responses. Someone who struggles with emotional control may find it hard to manage strong emotions. They may overreact, experience lasting bad moods, and get overwhelmed by the intensity of their feelings.

Movement control refers to the ability to control how and when the body moves. A person who has difficulty with movement control may experience restlessness and find it difficult to remain still.

A self-controlled person exhibits a great deal of will-power and personal control. They don't act impulsively and can regulate their emotions and actions effectively.

Importance of Self-Control

How important is self-control in your day-to-day life? A Stress in America survey conducted by the **American Psychological Association (APA)** found that 27% of respondents identified a lack of will-power as the primary factor keeping them from reaching their goals.4 The majority of people surveyed (71%) believed that self-control can be both learned and strengthened.

Researchers have found that people who have better self-control tend to be healthier and happier, both in the short term and in the long term.

In one influential experiment, students who exhibited greater self-discipline had better grades, higher test scores, and were more likely to be admitted to a competitive academic program. The study also found that when it came to academic success, self-control was a more important factor than IQ scores.

The benefits of self-control are not limited to academic performance. One long-term health study found that high levels of self-control during childhood predicted greater cardiovascular, respiratory, and dental health in adulthood, as well as improved financial status.

Examples of Self-Control

Setting goals to exercising regularly, eating a balanced diet, being more productive, giving up bad habits, and saving money are just a few actions requiring self-control. More examples of self-control include:

- Avoiding social media when you are at work so that it doesn't hurt your productivity
- Not purchasing something you want because you are trying to stick to a budget
- Skipping sweet treats because you are trying to reduce your sugar intake
- Managing your emotional response when someone does something that makes you feel angry or upset

Delaying Gratification

The ability to wait to get what you want, is an important part of self-control. People are often able to control their behavior by delaying the gratification of their urges.

For instance, someone who wants to attend an expensive concert might avoid spending their money on weekend shopping trips. They want to have fun, but they know that by waiting and saving their money, they can afford the exhilarating concert instead of the everyday mall trip.

Delaying gratification involves putting off short-term desires in favor of long-term rewards. Researchers have found that the ability to delay gratification is important not only for attaining goals but also for well-being and overall success in life.

The Marshmallow Test

Walter Mischel conducted a series of well-known experiments during the 1960s and 1970s that investigated the importance of delayed gratification. In these experiments, children were offered a choice: They could choose to eat one treat right away (usually a cookie or a marshmallow), or they could wait a brief period of time in order to get two treats.

At this point, researchers would leave the child alone in a room with a single treat. Not surprisingly, many of the kids chose to eat the single treat the moment the experimenters left the room. However, some of the kids were able to wait for the second treat.

Researchers found that children who were able to delay gratification in order to receive a greater reward were also more likely to have better academic performance than the kids who gave in to temptation immediately.

The "Hot-and-Cool" System

Based on his research, Mischel proposed what he referred to as a "hot-and-cool" system to explain the ability to delay gratification. The hot system refers to the part of our will-power that is emotional and impulsive and urges us to act upon our desires. When this system takes over, we may give in to our momentary desires and act rashly without considering the potential long-term effects.

The cool system is the part of our will-power that is rational and thoughtful and enables us to consider the consequences of our actions in order to resist our impulses. The cool system helps us look for ways to distract us from our urges and find more appropriate ways to deal with our desires.

The ability to delay gratification is linked to a number of benefits, including better goal attainment and positive life outcomes. Finding ways to distract yourself from temptation can help you strengthen your ability to delay gratification.

Ego Depletion

Research has found that self-control is a limited resource. In the long term, exercising self-control tends to strengthen it. Practicing self-control allows you to improve it over time. However, self-control in the short term is limited.

Focusing all of your self-control on one goal makes it more difficult to exercise your self-control on subsequent tasks throughout your day.

Psychologists refer to this tendency as ego depletion. This happens when people use up their reservoir of willpower on one task, making them unable to muster any self-control to complete the next task.

Health Benefits of Self-Control

Self-control is also important for maintaining healthy behaviors. What you eat for breakfast, how often you work out, and whether you have a consistent sleep schedule are all decisions that can be affected by your levels of self-control.

Researchers have found that self-control can have a number of potential influences on health and well-being. One longitudinal study found that adults who had greater self-control in childhood were less likely to have:

- Airflow obstruction
- Elevated inflammation
- Metabolic abnormalities
- Periodontal disease
- Sexually transmitted infections
- Substance dependence or addiction to tobacco, alcohol, or cannabis

While it is clear that self-control is critical for maintaining healthy behaviors, some experts believe that overemphasizing the importance of willpower can be damaging.

The belief that self-control alone can help us reach our goals can lead people to blame themselves when their health is influenced by factors beyond their control. It may also lead to feelings of learned helplessness. If people feel that they cannot do anything to change a situation, they may give up quickly or simply stop trying in the face of obstacles.

Motivation and Monitoring

According to psychologist and researcher Roy Baumeister, lack of will-power is not the only factor that affects goal attainment. If you are working toward a goal, three critical components must be present:

- There needs to be a clear goal and the motivation to change. Having an unclear or overly general goal (such as "getting stronger") and insufficient motivation can lead to failure. You are more likely to achieve a clearly defined goal with a specific motivation.
- You need to track your actions toward the achievement of the goal. Simply setting the goal is not enough. You need to monitor your behavior each day to ensure that you are doing the things that need to be done in order to reach your goal.
- You need to have will-power. Being able to control your behavior is a critical part of achieving any goal. Fortunately, research suggests that there are steps people can take in order to make the most of their available will-power.

Will-power alone doesn't determine whether or not you will reach a goal. A range of other factors, including your motivation and ability to monitor your progress, also play a critical role.

How to improve Self-Control?

While research suggests self-control has its limitations, psychologists have also found that it can be strengthened with certain strategies.

Avoid temptation

This is an effective way of making the most of your available self-control. Avoiding temptation ensures that you do not "use up" your available self-control before it is really needed.

Whether it's the desire to eat, drink, spend, or indulge in some other undesired behavior, one way to avoid temptation is to find a healthy distraction.

Go for a walk, call a friend or do whatever it takes to get your mind off whatever is tempting you at the moment.

Plan ahead

Consider possible situations that might break your resolve. If you are faced with temptation, what actions will you take to avoid giving in? Research has found that planning ahead can improve will-power even in situations where people have experienced the effects of ego depletion.

For example, if you are trying to reduce your sugar intake and you have a hard time controlling late afternoon hunger pangs, eat a well-balanced lunch packed with plenty of fiber, protein, and whole grains that will keep you full longer.

Practice using self-control

While your control might become depleted in the short term, regularly engaging in behaviors that require you to exert self-control will improve your will-power over time. While hard work may exhaust the muscle in the short term, the muscle will grow stronger over time as you continue to work it.

Focus on one goal at a time

Setting a lot of goals at once is usually an ineffective approach. Depleting your will-power in one area can reduce self-control in other areas. It is best to choose one specific goal and focus your energy on it.

Once you turn the behaviors needed to reach a goal into habits, you will not need to devote as much effort toward maintaining them. You can then use your resources to work on other goals.

Meditate

Meditation is a great way to strengthen your self-control muscle. If you're new to meditation, mindfulness meditation is a great place to start learning how to be more self-aware so you can better resist temptations. This technique can also help you learn to slow your thoughts, which can help you control the gut impulses that can get in the way of your self-control.

Remind yourself of the consequences

Just like self-control can help you achieve your goals and improve your physical and mental health, a lack of self-control can have adverse effects on your self-esteem, education, career, finances, relationships, and overall health and well-being. Reminding yourself of these consequences can help you stay motivated as you work to increase your self-control.

You can improve your own self-control with effort and practice. Avoiding temptations, making a plan, focusing on specific goals, and remembering the consequences of your actions can help you regulate your behavior more effectively.

Self-control refers to your ability to manage your behavior in order to achieve goals, improve positive outcomes, and avoid negative consequences. Self-control is an important skill that allows us to regulate behavior, and it is vital for attaining goals While self-control is a limited resource, there are things that you can do to improve and strengthen your will-power over time.

Chapter 10

How to develop Self-Discipline?

When you have the determination to improve self-discipline, you open up many doors to new opportunities. But it takes more than will-power to improve your ability to discipline yourself. You need to develop skills through learning and training yourself to practice self-control until being self-disciplined becomes a habit.

Given below are seven steps:

Step one: Decide what you want

The first step to improving your self-discipline is to organize your thoughts and figure out what you want. As Napoleon Hill puts it in one of his self-discipline quotes: "Self-discipline begins with the mastery of your thoughts. If you don't control what you think, you can't control what you do. Simply, self-discipline enables you to think first and act afterward."

Decide exactly what it is you want in each part of your life. Do you need to increase your knowledge of the trends in your industry so you can advance to a higher position? Do you want to adopt healthy habits like exercising and healthy eating so you feel better, increase your self-confidence, and open yourself up to more opportunities? Is learning a new language or skill something you want to do to open new doors professionally or personally?

Tap into your self-awareness and think about what you want to do and be. What decisions do you need to make today in order to start moving toward the top of your field? Whatever it is, make a decision now and then get started. This single act alone can change the whole direction of your life.

Understand that any new endeavor you take on will take effort and a willingness to delay gratification. But enduring temporary discomfort is always worth the reward of long-term gain.

Step two: Identify and remove temptations

Distractions are the enemy of accomplishment and discipline. Your ability to resist temptation will turn bad habits into good habits. One of the wisest things you can do to resist temptations is to simply remove temptations as much as possible.

If checking your social media has become a time-waster, reduce your screen time by setting limits on your smartphone, turning off notifications, scheduling specific times when you can check your accounts, or deleting the apps that do not contribute to your goals or overall well-being.

If you are easily distracted by how readily accessible entertainment is, remove things like television, video platforms, or subscription streaming services from your environment. Do the same with tempting foods, people that are a negative influence, or anything else that is impeding your progress.

Being honest with yourself about what those distractions are is key to your success. Fewer distractions have a tremendous impact on accomplishing your goals. Over the next several days, keep track of what you do all day. Writing it down will allow you to analyze how you spend your time and change it into how you want to spend your time.

As Harvey Dorfman puts it, "Self-discipline is a form of freedom. Freedom from laziness and lethargy, freedom from the expectations and demands of others, freedom from weakness and fear — and doubt."

Step three: Find an accountability partner

Sometimes it's hard to stay disciplined when you're working in silence. Having someone to share your goals and keep you accountable can help keep you on track and motivated to stay disciplined.

An accountability partner can help you overcome the challenge of making the changes you need to restrain your impulses and make better decisions. Setting a specific goal makes you 10% more likely to achieve it. But committing to someone else that you will do it increases your success rate by 65%, and making an appointment to report back to that person raises it even higher to 95%.

An accountability partner is someone with whom you make an agreement to help each other stay on track toward achieving your goals. In your effort to improve self-discipline, knowing that you need to report your actions to someone else will help you stay motivated, and you will do the same for them.

An ideal accountability partner is someone who is working toward similar goals as you. For example, if your goal is to start your own business, choose an accountability partner who shares the same entrepreneurial goal. In this way, you can learn together, brainstorm solutions, and share helpful insights on the training each other is receiving.

You should also choose someone who wants to be held accountable — a person as interested in building self-discipline as you are. The right accountability partner is trustworthy and will keep your discussions confidential. They are kind and encouraging yet will also ask you difficult questions and give constructive criticism to help you stay on track.

Share your goals with your accountability partner, be honest about your progress, and stay connected regularly. Set daily, weekly, and monthly check-in appointments, and keep these sessions short and on-topic. Communicate in a way both of you are comfortable with, such as email, text, phone calls, in-person meetings, or a combination of several modes of communication.

The positive reinforcement and encouragement you receive from your accountability partner — and in turn, give to them — can make all the difference in overcoming the roadblocks you have been experiencing and catapulting you toward making your hopes and dreams a reality.

Step four: Write your goals down

A goal that is not in writing is not a goal at all. It is merely a wish and it has no energy behind it. Write your goals down, clearly and in detail. The most successful goals are SMART goals: specific, measurable, achievable, relevant, and time-bound.

Define your long-term goals, but then set small goals and work your way to bigger ones. Baby steps are easier to visualize and achieve. They help you overcome your challenges more effectively than focusing on broad goals that take time to reach. Reaching your smaller goals will motivate you to continue on the road to progress.

If your goal is to eat healthier, for example, start by adding one new healthy food to your diet each week. You don't have to eliminate all unhealthy food at once. Going slowly will help you stay motivated.

It takes a tremendous amount of will-power to make a sweeping change all at once. But making gains step-by-step will be training your mind to exercise self-control in manageable increments until it becomes a habit and you no longer have the desire to return to old ways.

Step five: Make to-do lists

Keep yourself on track daily by making a to-do list of everything you can think of that you are going to have to do to accomplish your goal. This is one of the most important things you can do to help you be productive and feel happier.

Lists serve as visual reminders that you are on a path toward excellence. Checking off each task as you complete it provides instant motivation to keep moving forward.

When you think of new tasks and activities, write them on your list until your list is complete. Revisit your goals regularly to make sure you are on track. If you need to change a word or sentence in your goal to make it more precise, relevant, or achievable, do so without compromising your progress. The key is to create and follow goals that will get you closer to the existence you want, never farther away.

At the end of each day, make your list for the next day. Small habits like this will keep your mind focused on taking the right actions toward exercising self-control. Be sure to set deadlines for all of your goals and sub-goals. This will help you work hard and achieve results in a timely manner.

Step six: Organize your lists

Organize your lists into a plan. Decide what you will have to do first and what you will have to do second. Decide what is more important and what is less important. And then write out your plan on paper, the same way you would develop a blueprint to build your dream house.

Group the tasks on your list into related items. This will help you save time and effort if you complete similar items in the same time period. Your mind will be in tune and your workspace will be organized with what you need.

Avoid multitasking. While it may seem like you are busy doing more, multitasking actually serves as a distraction as you cannot devote the right amount of mental energy to a single task. Tackle one item at a time then move on to the next one.

Step seven: Create an action plan

Do something every single day that moves you in the direction of your most important goal at the moment. Develop the time management discipline of doing something 365 days each year that is moving you forward. You will be absolutely astonished at how much you accomplish when you utilize this formula every single day.

Chapter 11

Stories on Self-Discipline

'The Tiger' – An Inspiring Story by Remez Sasson

A teacher and his student were walking from one village to another, when all of a sudden, they heard a roar behind them. They turned their head in the direction of the roar, and saw a big tiger following them.

The student was horrified, and the first thing he wanted to do was to run away, but since he had been studying and practicing self-discipline, he was able to stop himself from running, and wait to see what his teacher would do.

"What shall we do master?" Asked the terrified student.

The teacher looked at the student and answered in a calm voice:

"There are several options. We can fill our minds with paralyzing fear so that we cannot move, and let the tiger do with us whatever pleases it. We can also run away, but then, the tiger will run after us and catch us."

"Another option is to fight, but this is not a good option, since the tiger is stronger than us. We can pray to God to save us, and we can also send the tiger our love."

"There is another thing we can do. We can choose to influence the tiger with the power of our mind. However, this requires strong concentration."

"We can focus and meditate on the inner power that are within us, and on the fact that we are one with the entire Universe, including the tiger, and in this way influence its soul."

"Which option do you choose?" Asked the frightened student. You are the master. You tell me what to do. We don't have much time."

The master turned his gaze fearlessly toward the tiger, emptied his mind from all thoughts, and entered a deep state of meditation. In his consciousness, he embraced everything in the Universe, including the tiger.

In this state the consciousness of the teacher became one with the consciousness of the tiger.

Meanwhile the student started to shiver with fear, as the tiger was already quite close, ready to make a leap at them. He was amazed at how his teacher could stay so calm and detached in the face of danger.

Meanwhile, the teacher continued to meditate without fear.

After a while the tiger gradually lowered its head and tail, turned around, and went away.The student was astonished and asked his teacher, "What did you do?" "Nothing. I just cleared all thoughts from my mind and united myself in spirit with the tiger. We became united in peace on the spiritual level."

"The tiger sensed the inner calmness, peace, and unity and felt no threat or need to display violence."

"When the mind is silent and calm, its peace is automatically transmitted to everything and everyone around, influencing them deeply," concluded the teacher.

About the Author

Remez Sasson is the author and creator of **Success Consciousness website**. He is the author of books and articles that motivate and help people to improve their life, achieve success, gain inner strength and inner peace, and become more positive and happy.

Chapter 12

Stories on Self-Discipline contd...

'Discipline is the Key to Success'

Once upon a time, there was a young boy named Jack. He was a bright and ambitious child, eager to make something of himself in the world. However, Jack had a problem: he was not very disciplined. He would often delay on his homework and chores, preferring to play video games or hang out with friends instead.

As Jack grew older, this lack of discipline began to hold him back. He struggled in school, often failing to turn in assignments on time. He had trouble keeping a part-time job, as he would often arrive late or take long breaks. He even had trouble maintaining friendships, as he would often cancel plans at the last minute.

One day, Jack realized that his lack of discipline was preventing him from achieving his goals. He knew that if he wanted to succeed in school, in his career, and in life, he needed to make a change. He decided to start implementing some discipline into his daily routine.

He began by setting small goals for himself. He would start by waking up earlier in the morning and making his bed. He would then set a goal for how much homework he would complete before allowing himself to play video games. He would make a schedule for his day and stick to it.

At first, it was difficult for Jack to stick to his new routine. He would often find himself getting distracted and falling back into old habits. But he was determined to change, so he kept pushing himself.

Over time, Jack began to see the benefits of his discipline. His grades improved, and he was able to earn better scholarships and get accepted into a better college. He was able to hold down a steady job, and even got a promotion. His friendships improved as well, as he was able to be more reliable and dependable.

Years went by, and Jack graduated from college with honors. He landed a good job in his field and started climbing the ladder of success. He had a good reputation at work, and his boss trusted him with more responsibilities. He had a good circle of friends and family who supported him.

Jack realized that discipline was the key to his success. He had worked hard and sacrificed a lot to get where he was, but it was all worth it. He was proud of what he had accomplished and knew that he could achieve anything he set his mind to. He continued to work hard and maintain his discipline, knowing that it was the key to his continued success.

The moral of the story is that discipline is the key to success. It may be hard to stick to a routine at first, but the rewards are well worth it in the end. With discipline, you can achieve your goals and make something of yourself in the world. So, if you want to succeed, remember to be disciplined and stay focused on your goals.

Chapter 13

The story of Discipline and Life Purpose

Three young men were going through the woods on a bright sunny day. These men were wonderful buddies, and they all had ambitious goals in life. John, Kevin and Frank were their names.

As the friends were chatting about their goals, talking about pretty girls, and cracking jokes, Kevin suddenly fell into the Earth with a yelp!

John and Frank ran over to the hole where Kevin fell.

John yelled, "Oh my gosh Kevin! Are you okay?"

Kevin replied weakly, "Yeah, I think so... can you guys help me get out of here?"

Frank and John grabbed Kevin and pulled him up.

"Thanks, guys, I thought I was a goner for a second there. What is this hole?"

Frank pulled out a pocket flashlight and shined the light down the hole.

"I think it's a well," said Frank.

John muttered, “Well jeez, I saw a danger warning sign or something was telling you that there was a well smack dab in the middle of the forest path.”

Suddenly, a sign appeared in front of the three friends that read, “DANGER! Magical Well Ahead. Watch your step!”

Frank, John, and Kevin were flabbergasted. They could not believe their eyes.

Kevin exclaimed, “No way! This has got to be a dream. So basically this is a real-life wishing well? I thought this stuff only happened in the movies.”

The other two friends murmured in agreement.

Frank decided to take a chance of looking like a fool and wished for an apple.

An apple appeared in front of them out of nowhere.

When the other two buddies realised what was going on, they made their wishes as well.

Kevin wants a gorgeous lady to take out on a date, while John wishes for a new bicycle.

A black gear bicycle and a lovely young woman emerged out of nowhere.

Frank stood passively watching as John rode around on his new bicycle while Kevin struck up a flirting chat with his new girlfriend. He could tell something wasn't quite right.

His father had always warned him that if something seemed too good to be true, it was most likely true.

By wishing in a well, no one gets anything for nothing. There had to be a catch, Frank thought.

Just as that thought bubbled up in his mind, John yelled as he crashed into the bushes while riding the cycle.

The bike had disappeared out from underneath him! Kevin’s new lady friend also disappeared into thin air, which left him disappointed as things were coming along quite well for him up until that moment.

“What the heck happened? My new bike vanished!” exclaimed John.

Frank checked his watch.

"Guys, you've been making your wishes for exactly 30 minutes. I believe you should try again in 30 minutes and see if it happens again.”

John and Kevin made their same respective wishes again. This time, nothing happened.

“Maybe we can’t make the same wish twice or something? I wish for a sports car!” said John.

Almost instantly, a shiny red Ferrari appeared before him.

“Sweet!” said John.

Feeling depressed about losing his new girlfriend, Kevin wished for his favourite junk food, sat down, and started eating.

Again, Frank wished for nothing more, wanting to see what would happen again after 30 minutes.

Lo-and-behold, in another 30 minutes John fell to the ground and gained a few scratches and bruises.

Luckily, the Ferrari was parked when the 30 minutes were up! John had just been sitting inside.

After making sure his friend was okay, Frank turned to Kevin and asked, “Kevin, does your stomach feel any lighter?”

"No, I can still feel the food in my stomach," Kevin said, having long since finished his dinner. I suppose if you eat whatever you want before the 30 minutes are over, you get to keep it!"

The three pals would return to the well together over the next few weeks.

Kevin and John wished for more and more things that they’ve always wanted but didn’t feel they could get without the magic of the well.

Frank did end up making a few wishes and had some fun, but quickly grew dissatisfied.

He accompanied the other two friends less frequently as time passed.

Frank observed that his friends stopped talking about their goals and plans for the future as much as they had in the past.

Now, all they could think about was what they were going to wish for next from the magical well.

As time went on, Frank grew more distant from Kevin and John. Noticing this Kevin and John confronted Frank and asked him why he was spending less time with them.

"You folks think this well is a wonderful treasure," Frank explained, "but all I see is fool's gold." None of the things we wish for here endures very long, and I believe you're beginning to get addicted. Plus, if you don't work for what you have, you won't appreciate it as much, and you won't take enough breaks from the nonstop indulgence."

Kevin, who had acquired weight as a result of all the food he had requested, responded, "Fine then." Max, you're free to do as you choose. We don't need you or your stuffy principles as long as we have this magical well here."

John nodded. "We have everything we need," says the narrator. Sure, it doesn't last very long, but we may keep hoping for things and never have to deal with the stress of hard work. Why put up the effort if you don't have to?"

Frank tried to warn his friends of the hidden dangers of the magic well, but they refused to listen.

At that moment, Frank bid his lifelong friends farewell, as there was nothing more he could do to convince them.

He began walking away, all alone.

For the next couple of decades, Frank went to work.

His mastery of discipline allowed him to have complete control over himself and his appetites.

Although he was a very successful and influential man who could have nearly anything he wanted, have a beautiful house, cars but he rarely over-indulged himself.

He enjoyed incredible experiences that came with his wealth, but he did so in moderation, balancing pleasure with disciplined effort.

One morning, Frank found himself feeling guilty. On a sunny day, he was in his backyard, overlooking a beautiful blue ocean sea, with his gleaming white house proudly standing behind him.

He was thinking about his friends from all those years ago as he gazed into the water. He felt like he'd abandoned them, so he decided to go to the woods.

He knew he'd have to wait a long time for them to come around to the magical well because he didn't know if they still lived near it or even if they still frequented it as frequently as they used to.

Despite this, he packed his camping gear and drove to the woods. He carefully stepped onto the route after parking his red Bentley SUV outside the trees.

Suddenly, an old-looking man with a long beard and dark eye bags under his eyes appeared from the bushes.

He was smelly, extremely skinny, dirty-looking, and seemed to be wearing rags.

"M-Frank?" whimpered John.

At Frank appeared confused, but then his expression quickly changed to one of pure horror. "Oh my god, John, is that you?"

After a tense conversation with John, Frank discovered that John and Kevin had moved into the woods to be closer to the well several decades ago.

They'd become completely entangled with what it could do for them. The longer they stayed with the well, the more dependent they became on it.

Since everything they wished for disappeared in 30 minutes, they had nothing to show for the years they spent in the woods, which was in complete contrast to Frank.

Not only that, but they never acquired key virtues like patience, diligence, gratitude and discipline because they never had to labour for what the well gave.

The magic well sent both Kevin and John into a downward spiral of self-destruction for many years.

Unfortunately, John informed Frank that Kevin had passed away many years ago from complications caused by all the unhealthy food and drink he addictively wished for.

John did not know how to cope with the loss of his friend and felt that he couldn't integrate himself back into society, so he decided to live out the rest of his life in the woods.

Over the years, John had grown tired of wishing for things that only destroyed his body and mind further.

He began to wish for tools and nature literature from the well to learn how to live off the land naturally and be free of its terrifying influence.

Frank and John spent the rest of the day together catching up, although it wasn't exactly a joyous reunion.

At the end of the day, Frank invited John to come to stay with him until he could transition back into society, but John vehemently refused.

As Frank turned to leave and return home, John called, "You were right you know. All those years ago, you tried to warn us, Frank. Like fools, we tried to take immediate gratification without putting in the discipline to create truly lasting rewards in our lives. I realize it now. If we had listened, maybe Kevin would still be with us."

Frank froze after hearing John's words. Unsure of what to say, Frank continued walking towards his car with tears rolling down his face.

The moral of the story is that nothing worthwhile in life is possible without self-discipline.

In our own lives, the "magic well" might take numerous shapes. For some, it may emerge as a never-ending search for a "get-rich-quick" scheme. It could be an addiction to television, video games, or partying for others. For others, it could be chasing the opposite sex all the time.

All of these things, like Frank, Kevin, and John's storey, might provide instant gratification, but they are all fleeting and ephemeral.

If you want to be truly successful, you must eliminate all "magic wells" in your life and devote yourself to the development of self-discipline via actual practice. There is no other option.

(Source: spiritual success.in)

Chapter 14

How to be Disciplined at the workplace?

Before we look into the qualities of a disciplined person, let's see the difference between self-discipline and self-control. Self-control allows us to control our behavior and avoid temptations. Self-discipline encourages us to do activities we should be doing, even when we don't feel like doing them. While self-control takes care of our short-term goals, self-discipline gets us through our long-term goals. Self-control and self-discipline are like two buddies who always work together.

What are the qualities of a disciplined person?

The most significant qualities of a self-disciplined person are:

1. Responsibility,
2. Persistence,
3. Strong work ethic, and
4. Self-care.

Let's understand these qualities one by one.

Responsibility

How strong is your sense of responsibility? In order to answer this question, you'll need to think about whether you get to work on time and whether you give your best efforts to complete tasks on time. A sense of responsibility also means that it's up to you to start your assignments and finish them before the deadline.

Once you develop a sense of responsibility, it'll be much easier to move, deal with your workload, and complete everything you need to do. As you know, nobody's going to take your hand and force you to start doing your tasks, so you'll have to do it yourself. That's why being responsible for your work is important if you want to be a self-disciplined employee.

Persistence

Have you ever thought about how marathon runners manage to run so many miles? They train themselves in order to build endurance.

In a workplace, endurance is called persistence. As a self-disciplined employee, you need to build your persistence. Therefore, you'll be able to motivate yourself to work not only 30 minutes per day, but longer. Persistence also helps you stay focused on your assignments for prolonged periods.

Now, apart from time frames of focused work, you should always remember to take frequent breaks. There's no point in working for 10 hours without any rest because this routine will drain your energy. Instead, train yourself to work for eight hours and include lunch and other brief breaks to refresh your mind.

Strong work ethic

When it comes to being self-disciplined at work, it's important to mention a trait such as a strong work ethic. In a way, you can say that responsibility plays a key role in creating a strong work ethic.

- Showing up for work on time.
- Dealing with all tasks, including both complex and less complex ones. An employee with a strong work ethic will tackle less interesting assignments, as well.
- Getting the job done. When people have a strong work ethic, they deliver all tasks on time.

Having a strong work ethic isn't always easy, which is why you'll need to be self-disciplined. Besides, you'll sometimes have to deal with distractions and stay strong when interruptions occur.

Self-care

Being self-disciplined also means taking care of yourself. When it comes to self-care, we have to emphasize the importance of sleep. Since sleep deprivation can weaken your self-control, people who are disciplined make sure they get enough sleep.

Apart from sleep, self-care equals making healthier choices regarding smoking, diet, and exercise. That's why researchers have proven that people who practice self-care are healthier in the long term, thanks to making proper choices about their health.

How do you improve self-discipline at workplace?

Are you struggling with self-discipline at work? Here are some invaluable tips to improve your self-discipline.

Start with small self-control exercises

Roy F. Baumeister is a social psychologist and the co-author of **Willpower: Rediscovering the Greatest Human Strength**. In his opinion, we should understand self-control as a strength. "It's like a muscle that you exercise."

Baumeister further explains. "Pick one fairly easy improvement in your life and execute it. For example, you could make your bed each morning. Or make sure to clean up all the dishes right after meals."

Baumeister also points out that we should use self-control to break bad habits and form good ones. For instance, by starting a regular daily practice of exercise, or meditation. Here's why he believes this is important: "Once something becomes a habit, it is no longer a self-control exercise. When I started jogging, I had to push myself to do it, and so it strengthened my self-control. By now it is a long-established daily habit, so doing it no longer qualifies as self-control building."

Moreover, Baumeister adds that jogging itself may require self-control, such as keeping going when tired. Therefore, you'll need self-discipline as well, to continue with a habit when you don't feel like doing it.

How can you try this routine at work? Here's one way: pick a task you don't particularly like, such as checking your inbox in the morning. Even though you don't enjoy it, do this task first thing you get to the office. Then, make yourself a cup of coffee, as a little treat. After a week or two, you'll notice how this assignment has become your daily habit, which you might even enjoy.

Break one large task into several small assignments

When you have one complex task on your plate, you may feel confused. You probably won't know how to start and what segment of your task to tackle first.

To prevent such situations, it's best if you break that assignment into several smaller ones. That way, you'll find it easier to complete the first task, and you'll be motivated to continue with others. Besides, this motivation will help you improve your self-discipline because you'll manage to complete all assignments on time.

Avoid multitasking

We tend to believe that juggling several tasks at once will help us finish our work faster. But, in reality, when we switch between tasks (multitasking), we can only focus on task 1. At the same time, task 2 is just a distraction to task 1.

As we mentioned earlier, self-discipline helps you maintain your focus on work assignments for a longer time. Therefore, to aim your attention on one task at a time, you should avoid multitasking.

Take breaks

If we perceive our self-control as a muscle, as Baumeister suggests, we can train our self-control. But, there should be limits here, too. When you train your self-control and self-discipline without any break, you'll feel exhausted.

The solution is quite simple: take regular breaks from work. By doing so, it's more likely that you'll regain your focus after a brief period of rest.

Moreover, you should schedule your breaks to ensure that you don't miss any. This is especially important on the days when you have to tackle a complex task, after which you're tired. In these situations, you can schedule a longer break after you finish that dreadful task.

Try to fight distractions

Another way to build your self-discipline is to avoid workplace distractions at any cost. Whenever you're dealing with tedious tasks, it can be very tempting to pick up your phone and scroll down your social media accounts for 15 or 20 minutes. But, when you manage to fight this urge in order to finish your task on time, you'll enhance your self-control (short-term win) and your self-discipline (long-term win).

So, how can you stay focused at work in a world full of distractions? If you usually lose focus because of various noises, invest in a pair of noise-canceling headphones. Or, if your mobile phone is your number one distraction, be sure to leave it out of reach when you're working.

You can also write down what distracts your attention the moment you experience it. Keep a notebook nearby to note down various distractions, and you'll notice some patterns. Thus, it'll be easier for you to figure out how to predict these interruptions and create order in your daily work tasks.

Create a productive environment

If you'd like to improve your self-discipline at work, you can also make a productive environment. That way, you'll send signals to your brain that it's time to focus on work tasks. It doesn't even have to be anything too demanding. For example, you can go get a glass of water before you start working on an assignment. Then, once you begin your task, be sure to aim all your attention at work. After several days, this ritual will become a habit that your brain will associate with deep work. Therefore, you'll upgrade your self-discipline levels as well.

Reward yourself

The best way to motivate yourself to keep doing your tasks is to celebrate little wins. Whenever you finish a task, remember to reward yourself. It can be taking a brief break to make lemonade or eat a chocolate bar. Building self-discipline by doing demanding work and being persistent is almost painless when you know rewards are waiting for you.

Developing self-discipline when working from home

When working from home, you have to nurture your self-discipline. In work environments such as this, it's only up to you to get up on time every day and give your best to complete your tasks before the deadline.

Choose working hours and stick to the schedule

If you don't have fixed working hours, you get to choose when you'll work during the day. To develop self-discipline, you should select working hours that are suitable for you and your lifestyle. Then, try to stick to that schedule as much as you can. Of course, it won't be a problem if you start your workday at 9 am on Monday, but at 9.30 on Tuesday. Allow yourself some flexibility on the days when you have personal errands to run before or after work.

Choose work attire that helps you stay productive

When you work from home, should you dress like you're dressed in an office? Some studies have shown that dressing up can enhance your performance at work.

But, does it work for all people? Probably not. Some employees will likely enjoy wearing a suit when working from home. For them, this can have a positive effect on productivity. On the other hand, some workers will prefer comfy clothes when telecommuting. From my work from home experience, wearing the clothes that I usually wear at home works perfectly. Plus, it doesn't hinder my productivity, so I manage to complete my tasks on time.

The bottom line is: choose the outfit that works best for you. Opt for clothes that you feel comfortable in and that help you stay productive. Thus, you'll be able to maintain your focus at work for longer periods, which will improve your self-discipline.

Finish your workday by preparing for tomorrow

To ensure you'll leave your work on time, you should spend some time at the end of the day thinking about tomorrow. Since self-discipline means being able to get the job done, you should reflect on what you've accomplished throughout the day. Then, write down if there are some urgent tasks for tomorrow morning. Moreover, note down all priorities for the day ahead of you and break larger projects into smaller assignments. Creating a to-do list for tomorrow can help you organize your time at work better.

The most significant qualities of a self-disciplined person are responsibility, persistence, strong work ethic, and self-care. Even if you don't feel like you check all these boxes, be sure that developing your self-discipline is possible. This process starts with self-control exercises. Besides, other ways to enhance your self-discipline are avoiding multitasking and distractions, as well as creating a productive environment for yourself. Furthermore, making sure that you're disciplined is especially important when working from home. In that case, you should try to stick to your working hours at home, and always make plans for the day ahead of you.

Chapter 15

Self-Discipline skills for your career

Self-discipline skills are what makeS you reliable, so every employer is searching for employees who are strong in this area.

The following are some of the self-discipline skills that you need to develop to succeed in your career:

Concentration skills.

Concentration is the ability to direct your mind to focus on one thing without letting distractions sway you from your goal. It is an aspect of self-discipline because it enables you to focus on work even when no one is supervising you.

If you have good concentration skills you can follow through with your job tasks even when there is so much going on in your life.

Your life at home could be falling apart but you would still focus on what you need to do. And even if there is a crisis in the workplace, you can continue to work as you should while everyone is panicking.

Some of the jobs that need a heavy dose of concentration include surgery, firefighting, and air traffic control jobs.

Planning skills.

Planning is the process of coming up with the ideas and actions that are needed to achieve your goals.

Goal-setting is an important aspect of self-discipline. This process is meant to clarify for you what your intentions are and how success looks like. It may also include the strategies you can use to achieve that success. Good goals must be specific, measurable, attainable, relevant, and time-based.

Your goals will act as the big picture when you carry out tasks to reach where you want to be. And planning skills will be instrumental in determining how well you can implement those goals. Without these skills, your actions will be directionless.

Time management skills.

Everyone has 24 hours on any given day. What you do with that time will determine how productive you are. Your ability to manage your time efficiently and effectively is an indicator of whether you have great discipline.

The lack of discipline concerning time will show in the way you fail to meet your deadlines and your poor work performance within a set period.

You will delay and the work to be done will keep on piling up on your desk. Your co-workers and managers will consider you to be lazy and unreliable. And you may even get fired.

Stress management skills.

Stress management is the ability to control your level of stress to improve the way you function daily. How stressed you are on any given day will affect your ability to concentrate, quality of work, and productivity.

Self-disciplined people are good at managing stress so that it doesn't interfere with their performance at work. As a result, they tend to exhibit a huge level of self-control and are happier even when the situation they are in is not favorable.

Fitness skills.

Fitness skills refer to the ability to participate in sports and perform physically-challenging activities. It is a sign of good physical health.

To become fit, you need to engage in exercises regularly. You must also eat right so that you can maintain your ideal body weight and size.

Being fit will need you to make sacrifices. And when you are tired, in pain, and crave certain foods, you must still regulate your emotions .

Training your body regularly improves your discipline and control. To master your mind when you feel discomfort is difficult. But when you get done and you experience the rewards, you can pat yourself on the back for a job well done.

Some of the jobs that need disciplined people with high levels of fitness include the military, professional athletics, and construction work.

Communication skills.

Communication is the exchange of information through verbal and nonverbal cues. That means you should master what you say and how your body reacts lest you offend someone.

One important aspect of communication is active listening. This refers to the ability to hear and understand what someone says, remember, and respond appropriately.

You should be disciplined enough to follow instructions when you need to. But first, you must fully understand what information is being communicated to you.

And even when you feel that the instructions you are given are irrelevant, you must separate the negative emotions from your duties.

So, you must learn to control your words and body language and get things done even if you are reluctant to do so.

Motivational skills.

Motivational skills refer to the ability to initiate and maintain actions that enable you to achieve your goals.

You must be in control of your mind and emotions to encourage yourself to stick to your routines even when you feel bored. Your mastery over your feelings will be instrumental in helping you stay committed to your course of action to the end despite the obstacles on the way.

Your motivational skills will also help your co-workers continue to perform even when there are issues in the workplace. They will ensure you can control individual and team performances significantly to obtain the results you desire.

Leadership skills.

Leadership skills will enable you to influence people's behavior around you so that they can implement the desired ideas and actions.

Great leaders have a lot of self-discipline. They must be able to work hard without supervision because no one will tell them what to do. They must be able to self-regulate their emotions to influence the behaviors of others. That way, you will become a better manager.

Collaboration skills.

Collaboration skills enable you to work well with others to complete tasks and achieve the set goals.

People will not always agree. Everyone has an opinion. And different opinions can lead to disagreements and distractions that slow the team down. But if you discipline yourself you can work well with others and achieve your goals.

The more you learn to control your emotions despite how other people in your team behave the better you will become at self-control. And you will become the person everyone wants in their team because you can be relied upon to work well with your colleagues.

Writing skills.

There is no point in being disciplined if you don't know what you are working towards.

You can even go one step further and write down the processes and strategies you should use to achieve those goals. Breaking down your goals into smaller ones will help improve your progress. To-do lists for daily tasks will be helpful too.

It's easy to remember what you need to do if you write it down. You can refer to it whenever you need to so that you don't get off course.

Journaling will be instrumental in helping you put your thoughts on paper. That is a great way of understanding your thinking process, managing your emotions better, and improving your mental well-being.

The more in control of your emotions you are the more discipline you will have.

Organizational skills.

Organizational skills refer to your ability to create structure and bring order to a situation. You must be able to plan what to do, execute tasks to achieve goals, and ensure everything is done efficiently.

It's difficult to have self-discipline if you have no sense of organization. Because your organizational skills will be needed to prioritize tasks, delegate duties, and provide direction so that you can work hard to achieve success. And they will help you do these activities with minimal supervision.

Critical thinking skills.

Critical thinking is the ability to analyze and evaluate a situation before deciding on the wisest course of action.

For example, if you are hell-bent on losing weight, you can think critically about what would happen if you rewarded yourself with junk food or stopped going to the gym. Once you decide that you are better off with less weight, in the long run, you will withstand discomfort better when exercising.

To self-regulate successfully, you must be a critical thinker. You should analyze what each course of action will lead to by weighing the consequences carefully. Then depending on the options before you, you can use the best strategy to achieve your goal even if it's challenging.

Critical thinking can boost your ability to solve problems in the organization efficiently. It will make you an asset to any organization you work in.

Visualization skills.

Visualization is the ability to create images in your mind concerning a particular subject.

Sometimes a project or goal can be so big that your mind finds it difficult to grasp it fully. So, by visualizing it, you prepare your mind and body to embrace the idea completely. It helps to make the impossible quite possible. Think of it as a coping mechanism for the tough times.

Every time you feel like giving up on a difficult project, you can imagine what it will be like when it's complete. You could picture your happiness, that bonus check, or the awards that will come your way once you succeed.

That makes it easier for you to stick to the plan when you deal with the challenges along the way. You can stay motivated as you act to achieve your goals.

Persistence skills.

Persistence skills are a skill that enables you to stay on course when you are delayed or forced to overcome difficulties along the way.

You should be able to continue to perform your tasks even when you find them hard to do. And if you fail to meet your objectives, you must dust yourself up, learn from your mistakes, and continue working.

You must endure becoming self-disciplined. It's the only way to overcome failure.

Mindfulness skills.

Mindfulness skills refer to your ability to be self-aware. It enables you to acknowledge your thoughts and feelings without making any judgments. It also influences your ability to be present.

You need mindfulness skills to work on your tasks effectively because they keep you alert. These skills will also enable you to control your emotions and relax your body when you feel stressed out. You are less likely to feel overwhelmed as a result. Thus, your concentration levels and productivity will improve.

Technical skills.

Technical skills are hard skills that require you to undergo practical training or class-based education so that you can perform specific tasks. You must be a good learner to acquire these skills.

These may include tasks within the scientific, mechanical, information technology, and mathematical sectors. Examples of jobs include programming, project management, and technical support jobs.

Technical skills can boost self-discipline. The more hands-on experience you have, the better you will get at doing your job. And you can have some control over your reactions and productivity even when something malfunctions. So, you need to practice as much as possible.

How to strengthen your Self-Discipline skills?

Choose one skill to focus on at a time. If you try to get better at all self-discipline skills at once, you'll just end up frustrated. Instead, choose one or two you really want to see improvement in, and set SMART (specific, measurable, attainable, relevant, and time-bound) goals around that one.

Identify what needs to change.

When you know what self-discipline skill you want to work on, identify what is hindering you from being excellent at it and what you need to do to get those obstacles out of the way.

For example, if your goal is to improve your stress management skills, take the time to notice when you feel especially stressed and when you feel relatively relaxed.

Did that yoga class you took that one time get rid of your chronic stress headache? Do you start feeling off-kilter whenever you check your email inbox?

Take baby steps.

When you know what obstacles you need to overcome in order to see an improvement in a skill, you can start to work on overcoming them.

Maybe your baby step to improving your stress management is to cut your coffee intake from four lattes a day to three, and then a few weeks later to two. Or, maybe it's to sign up for the yoga class or to train yourself to hide your phone in a drawer until you leave for work in the morning.

They may sound small and simple, but you will be surprised at how far these tiny steps will take you.

Celebrate your progress.

You'll quickly run out of motivation to improve your self-discipline skills if you don't stop to look at how far you've come and pat yourself on the back now and then.

Plan a reward for yourself for hitting a goal such as a meal at the new restaurant you've wanted to try, or simply keep track of your progress and let yourself appreciate how far you've come.

Your ability to regulate your emotions and behavior to achieve your goals despite challenges will boost your chances of being hired. Find a way to list it in your resume as a soft skill. It will also raise your chances of getting management positions. Focusing on self-development can help you become a more disciplined person.

Chapter 16

What is Self-Control in children?

Self-control allows children and adults to manage their thoughts, actions and emotions so they can get things done. Sitting still, waiting in line, taking turns — we all use self-control in ways that may seem simple. But self-control is a complex skill that develops over time. Children start building self-control when they're very young and keep developing it into their 20s. As children get older, they develop self-control in three areas:

Movement control so children aren't constantly moving in inappropriate ways

Impulse control so children put on "mental brakes" and stop and think before doing or saying something

Emotional control so children can keep going even when upsetting things happen

Having self-control helps children in all areas of life. But it's especially important when it comes to socializing. Being in control of their actions and reactions helps children fit in and make friends.

Chapter 17

Speech on Self- Discipline

The proper meaning of self-discipline is to control one's temper and resist the temptations within them. Also, try their best to make right decisions and do activities that would help one positively.

Self-discipline is a very important virtue and all humans should try to attain it to some extent. There are various ways in which one can attain that. Self-discipline varies from a person to another, as time changes.

First, I would want to show that how self-discipline is an essential virtue for all of us. Irrespective of the age, we all should have self-discipline in ourselves. Self-discipline is when you know to utilize your time properly. In some cases, when we are enjoying ourselves, we all have a tendency to immerse ourselves in a fit of happiness and relaxation. And, therefore, we try to choose the way to neglect the other various important works. We keep neglecting and delaying to do that work, which could have been completed a long time before, if we were a bit more serious and focused.

Talking about the proper focus, we frequently get distracted while doing some other things. Our mind and attention seems to wander off, and we completely forget what we were doing. With the help of self-discipline, it wouldn't be a problem like that. We need to try our very best to improve ourselves at every important moment. Improving ourselves is also a beneficial part of self-discipline.

Children need to learn proper discipline from a young age. We need to educate them about the basic ethics and mannerisms of a good human being. We have to show them to use polite speech including the things like saying "sorry," "please," " beg your pardon," and many more. Then things like, respecting your seniors and elders, helping others out at the time when they need your help.

Some people are brought up as a self-disciplined person, whereas, others have to put in some labor in the desire of achieving it. To become a self-discipline person, one should engage in the practice of meditation. Meditation helps to calm the mind of a person and to become a cool-tempered person. It helps you to control your innermost desires and urges and thus channeling your energy to the right path in life.

Hobbies can always help you to relieve your stress, and it is also a very good way to learn something new and fun. Try to go to bed early, or read a good book before going to bed instead of staying awake until the dawn. It's very bad for our mental and physical health.

Self-discipline is very important as it teaches us to be a better human and also to be the better versions of ourselves. To be a decent, caring, polite and loving person of the society. Self-love is also an essential part of the virtue called self-discipline. You are doing this not for others but for your own good.

Chapter 18

How to build Self-Discipline in sports?

Competing at a high level requires consistency. You need to be able to perform your best on a consistent basis. Self-discipline will make sure you are consistent. Why? Because in order to be consistent during games, you actually need to focus on being consistent with your training and your approach.

Self-Discipline in Sports

Self-discipline means doing and not doing certain things for the sake of improving and reaching a goal. So, as an athlete, this means doing all that you need to do, on a consistent basis, to help you become the best you can be .

And not only that...self-discipline also means not doing certain things. You know, those activities you may like to do, but that are actually holding you back from being your best.

Here are a few key ways self-discipline can be applied in terms of sports:

The first is training. Being self-disciplined means you train as much as you know you should. You don't need a coach, trainer, parent, or anyone else to remind you to train and hold you accountable to work hard. You do that yourself because you are disciplined.

Another way self-discipline pertains to sports is being disciplined during games in terms of your mindset. Are you good at managing your thoughts before, during, and after a game? Are you able to keep yourself composed following mistakes or bad calls? Having good control over your mindset takes self-discipline.

A third way self-discipline applies to sports is with your routines. These can be training routines, warm-up routine, pre-game routines, eating routine, and so on.

You need to be disciplined with your routines, since it is your routines that will lead to consistent outcomes on the field or court.

Why Self-Discipline is important for athletes?

High level competitors at any sport reach that level, not just because they have extraordinary skills, but also because they do the little things very well and consistently.

Self-discipline allows you to put forth the kind of consistent work required to reach your goals.

When you have strong self-discipline, you will work even on the days when your mind seems to be running all over the place.

That's why being self-disciplined is so important! Now, let's take a closer look at what self-discipline leads to.

5 benefits of strong self-discipline:

Creates good habits. Developing good habits is a great way to put yourself on the path to success. With self-discipline, it becomes easier to hold yourself accountable and create good habits.

Helps you focus. The ability to focus during games is crucial! Self-discipline helps you focus on the task at hand and work against any distractions you may be dealing with.

Increases self-confidence. As your self-discipline improves, a new sense of confidence will be felt. This will be due to the pride felt in mastering yourself, and the knowledge you now have. Being able to control your thoughts and emotions gives you confidence that cannot be gotten anywhere else.

Helps to achieve mastery in a skill. To become great at any sport, many hours of practice must be put forth. Such work takes great self-discipline to stick with. It requires you to force yourself to repeat a simple task over and over until a skill is mastered.

Overcomes procrastination. We often say we'll do something tomorrow, then tomorrow turns into the next day, and so on. Self-discipline provides you the power to overcome procrastination and do what you know must be done.

So, what can you do if you want to build your self-discipline? Here are four steps you can take to build your self-discipline today!

4 steps to develop self-discipline in sports

Step 1: Find your motivation

Motivation is what drives us to set goals, face challenges, and perform the necessary hard work. So, we must decide what our motivation is for wanting to develop stronger self-discipline.

To become a better player, you need to get stronger, faster, and refine your skills. The time needed to be put into each area, required immense amounts of self-discipline.

After school, I began weight training and then going to the baseball field to work on my skills. Over time, I became incredibly disciplined with my work-ethic. This was carried throughout my college years, and I continue to implement such focus and discipline in my life today.

Through my experience, I learned how important motivation is to self-discipline. If we have a reason to hold ourselves accountable then we will take the steps necessary. Then, through repetition, the self-discipline will become habitual and natural.

Motivation can be extrinsic or intrinsic.

Extrinsic Motivation

Extrinsic motivation is when you are driven by external desires and goals. When you're motivated extrinsically, you usually seek rewards or look to avoid punishment. Either way, the reason for performing an action is due to something outside of yourself.

Some examples include:

- Playing a sport to receive accolades.
- Training hard to win a championship.
- Practicing every day to get a scholarship.
- Playing your sport to make your parents happy.
- Working hard during practice so you don't get yelled at.
- Weightlifting because your coach requires you to.

Intrinsic Motivation

Intrinsic motivation is the opposite of extrinsic. Working towards a goal or achievement is driven completely by internal desires. If you display this motivation type, then the activity itself is the source of joy and fulfillment.

Rather than being motivated by an award or to avoid punishment, being able to perform the task is motivation enough. Think about those players who love to train, even if they're not being forced to (maybe this is even you). That is clear intrinsic motivation at work.

Here are some examples of intrinsic motivation:

- Playing a sport because you find it enjoyable and fun.
- Weightlifting and exercising to get stronger for yourself.
- Hustling in practice because of your passion for the game.
- Staying after a game to practice because you love the feeling of working hard.
- Playing your sport because the act brings you joy.
- Studying film because you love to learn.

This is the first step towards developing incredibly strong self-discipline. You must first determine the motivation behind wanting to build it in the first place.

Step 2: Take small steps

The second aspect of building strong self-discipline as an athlete is to begin taking small steps.

Do you remember where I mentioned my experience with self-discipline? It was in high school when I really began to develop the habit. Well, it wasn't something that happened all at once.

Over the course of months and years, I began to be more and more disciplined. It is something that I continue to work on today. The key behind it, though, is small steps over a long time period.

Our brains love habits and routines. This is both good and bad. It is good because it means that we can program our brain into a new routine and stick with it. But bad if we are stuck in a negative habit.

With self-discipline, you don't want to overwhelm yourself. If you do, then it will likely lead to failure and frustration. That is where small steps come into play.

You can also think of this as setting little goals for yourself. By doing this, over time you will become more and more self-disciplined. And the more you become disciplined, the more your motivation rises to keep progressing.

Step 3: Keep a discomfort journal

The third step in developing self-discipline is all about holding yourself accountable.

I'm sure you have heard people say that the first step towards progress is outside of our comfort zone. It really is the truth.

Building self-discipline is no different. It requires you to continually test yourself, pushing ever further outside what is comfortable.

But this is very difficult to do. Your mind wants to keep you safe, and the work that needs to be done can be perceived as dangerous. All kinds of excuses and reasoning will go on in your head.

To curb this, and make sure you are taking the steps towards building self-discipline, a journal can be kept. Not just any journal, but a discomfort journal!

What is a Discomfort Journal?

Basically, this is going to be a journal you keep every night or week, depending on your schedule. In it, you will write down what you did that pushed you out of your comfort zone. This can be training when you didn't want to, working on a new skill, running, or anything else.

By forcing yourself to perform certain activities, you will be developing your self-discipline. And the discomfort journal just helps you to hold yourself accountable.

The reason it is important to do things that make you uncomfortable is due to the discipline it takes to perform them.

Keeping yourself a journal to track progress is a great way to ensure that you are pushing yourself each and every day. Slowly building up that self-discipline.

Step 4: Practice saying 'NO'

'No' is a very underused word. We often feel guilty about telling others no, and we seldom tell ourselves no enough.

However, if you wish to build truly incredible self-discipline as an athlete, then 'no' must become a frequently used word in your vocabulary.

When thinking about saying 'no' in terms of building self-discipline, there are two facets. Saying 'no' to others and saying 'no' to yourself.

Saying 'No' to others

Constantly saying 'yes' to people can drain us. It can become a time-waster, and often we say yes just out of the fear of saying no. Through practicing saying 'no' to others you do yourself a huge favor. More time can be spent on your own training, dreams, and goals.

As you become more disciplined in saying 'no', you will begin to only do the things that line up with your ideals and goals. No more time will be wasted doing things that you do not want to do, just because you felt like saying 'yes' was the only option.

Saying 'No' to yourself

There are many distractions that can present themselves to us on a daily basis.

One of the toughest things to do is say 'no' to ourselves. Especially when it is saying 'no' to something pleasurable in favor of something we need to do (like running or lifting instead of hanging out with friends).

However, if you want to build self-discipline and be the best player you can be, then it is a habit you must adopt.

Do you want to eat healthier? You must say no to junk food. Do you want to train more? You must say no to watching tv after school or practice. Do you want to become more productive? You must say no to procrastination.

'No' is a powerful word that is incredible in working towards a goal. Begin saying 'no' to yourself daily and you will see your self-discipline rise.

Better self-discipline is something all athletes should strive to build. It will lead to more consistency and more success in your sport. You will find it easier to create new habits and focus. Self-confidence will grow. Skills can be mastered much easier, and procrastination overcome.

By following the four steps outlined above, you can begin building incredible discipline in yourself as an athlete.

Chapter 19

How to develop Self-Discipline for online learning?

Self-discipline is "doing what needs to be done when it needs to be done even when you don't feel like doing it." The COVID-19 pandemic has definitely changed the face of the education system by triggering a learning revolution and metamorphosing into a completely new domain.

As it turns out, the sudden switch from brick & mortar to virtual classrooms has been challenging for students as well as for the teachers. With so many distractions posed by online learning, students need to develop self-discipline to succeed.

Make a schedule

A schedule ensures discipline and oozes productivity. Make a schedule, divide your time judiciously between all subjects, set aside time for homework and assignments, and assign at least an hour for practice along with self- assessment. Do not forget to set a specific time for self-study. Additionally, keep a close check on test dates, assignment submissions, etc. and add them to your weekly calendar. Following a schedule will help you stay disciplined and aid in better time management.

Stay prganized

Just making a schedule on paper is not going to help you in any way. You need something more than that. The key to develop self-discipline lies in staying organized.Start by arranging everything you need in advance including books, notes, stationery, etc. before the commencement of your online class. Double check your internet connection so that you are not logged out amid an ongoing session. Do not forget to take notes during live classes as you would in any other class and organize them in a way that makes sense to you. Apart from that, follow your schedule, submit your assignments in time, do not miss any test, and avoid procrastination. By staying organized you can accomplish your targets as efficiently as possible.

Choose a suitable study space

Studying online requires both dedication and self-discipline. A proper study space provides you with a perfect learning environment. In order to optimize your studies, choose a study space that is comfortable and quiet, thereby allowing you to focus well. It should also be well-lit with a good internet connection, access to power, and free from distractions.

Avoid distractions

Just being online can be distracting for a lot of you. The key to avoid distractions is to remove all possible sources of distractions from your surroundings. Turn off all notifications on your smartphone as it can distract you and waste your time. Make sure any redundant tabs or chat windows are closed while you are studying online. Follow the guidelines issued by your teachers for live classes and make the most of your online learning experience.

Participate in discussions

Always remember that learning is a two-way process. And with online learning, it has become more important than ever to communicate. Active engagement in online classroom discussions, asking questions, and sharing your opinions is a vital part of enhancing communication. If you won't participate or ask doubts, your teachers won't be able to check your progress. Your teachers can simply guide and mentor you. So, don't rely on others to ask questions; be proactive and take the charge of your learning.

Stop procrastinating

In order to be self-disciplined, you need to stop putting off tasks until tomorrow as it will only build up the work, making it too hard to catch up. Whatever is taught in the online class, make it a point to revise it the same day. Do your homework and complete your assignments in time. If a task seems too overwhelming, break it into smaller tasks to make it less intimidating. This will also make it more manageable.

Give tests with integrity

Integrity is one of the most important qualities one requires towards developing self-discipline for online learning. Taking tests with integrity allows you to properly evaluate your performance. We know how big a temptation it can be to just open your books at home and write all the correct answers just to see a higher score in exams. Taking tests honestly helps you to analyse your mistakes and gradually improve upon them. Moreover, tests are a way for your teachers to determine what you have learned and how much you have understood the syllabus taught in classes. If you are not honest and cheat with your own learning, it will defeat the whole point of taking tests. In addition, you might slip into the habit and never develop necessary test-taking skills.

The only thing that online learning demands is absolute discipline. You need to understand that this is not vacation time for you. Take charge of your success by becoming self-disciplined. Remember, it is discipline not desire that determines your destiny. Developing a sincere attitude towards online learning will help you to achieve your academic goals. Mere motivation to do well won't be enough for shaping your career ahead. Active discipline and integrity are the real game-changers.

Chapter 20

How to build Self-Discipline to learn something new?

Learning a new skill is not just a passion, in fact it is scientifically proven that acquiring a new skill brings excitement inside the brain which keeps one happier and cheerful in everyday life. Our brain is like a muscle and just like every other muscle, you have to exercise it by learning something new. Unfortunately, one cannot learn a new skill within a day and so we often struggle with keeping up with the process and quit very soon. Learning a new skill requires self discipline and here are some tips on how to build self discipline to learn a new skill or to form a new habit.

1. Focus on the journey and not the destination

Five years ago, I picked up a guitar and decided to take guitar lessons. The thought of playing my favourite songs and performing in front of an audience filled my heart with an unbeatable enthusiasm. I knew I just wanted to do that. And guess what, today my guitar gathers dust at one isolated corner of my house. Tragic, isn't it?

But now that I think about it, I had glorified the final outcome so much that I failed to understand that the journey (practicing guitar) was a lot more important. I did not enjoy practicing notes, switching between chords was a big nightmare and I could not play as fast as those professional guitarists that I had idolized before I picked the guitar. The moral of the story is if you focus on creating a habit and make it measurable, the outcome will likely come as a result. So, the first step is to figure out the habits that will get you closer to your goal everyday.

2. Start with small habits

Whether you're trying to build a healthy lifestyle or trying to learn a musical instrument, be certain that results will not show overnight. The key is to build up gradually. Small habits are easy to incorporate and easy to build on to create larger changes over time. Trying to learn a musical instrument? Make it a habit each morning to practice the lesson you've learnt the day before, even if it's just for 15 minutes. After that, your only job is to not break the chain. It's important to pick a task that is small enough to follow everyday yet significant enough to make a difference. Once you build a habit, the results will automatically start showing.

3. Be consistent

Being consistent with your daily habits is the most difficult yet the most important part of learning something new. It will take the longest time because maintaining that self discipline to follow a routine – especially when it gets mundane, is where most people quit.

Commit to your efforts every single day and give yourself a significant amount of time to get better. If you start feeling bored, try to level up and make things interesting. Do not start doubting your abilities until you've been consistent with your habit for a long time. It's consistency above everything else.

4. Don't wait for it to "feel right"

Building self-discipline will never feel right. Learning something new and building a new habit will force you to make active (and often difficult) decisions which will always feel wrong. Your brain will try to resist the changes and make you feel uncomfortable. What should you do in such a situation? Embrace it. Embrace the fact that it will take a while for you to feel comfortable or feel right. If you keep waiting for the "right moment" to start, you will never get close to the final outcome you desire.

5. Challenge your limitations

Doing something new will always challenge you and your brain will try to resist it. It will start coming up with excuses, sometimes so logical that you'll instantly be convinced to quit what you've started and go back to your existing routine. When stuck in such a situation - simply do not settle. Try finding out solutions, start questioning those "logical" excuses or rather be weird & illogical. If you've got to build self discipline to learn something new, you have to force yourself to make a mindset shift.

6. Stop caring about what "others will say"

Building self-discipline means that instead of finding approval from outside, you need to find approval within yourself. While learning something new, a lot of people quit halfway because they fear getting mocked by others. So when you start learning something new, do it only for yourself. Let go of the need for approval from others and focus on creating small consistent habits to achieve your goal.

7. Reward your progress

We often get so obsessed with achieving our final goal that we do not appreciate all the progress we've made. Even if you're not even close to your goal, the fact that you've made some progress from where you started is a reason to celebrate in itself. This gives even a bigger reason to make small measurable goals. Even if it feels silly as an adult, the rewards system is an effective tool to keep you consistent on the path to achieving your goals.

Chapter 21

How to improve your Interpersonal Skills?

It's important that you are able to understand the true nature of the area you wish to improve , if you are to accomplish anything at all.

The prefix of interpersonal is "inter" and inter means "in-between", hence interpersonal means in between people. Therefore, interpersonal skills are related to the activities that happen between people as they interact: how we speak, how we behave, how we respond to other people mentally and intellectually so that we are improving and creating desirable outcomes as a result of that interaction.

We interact with people every day. It could be people at work, at home, or even people across the world on social media. But how do you ensure that interaction with other people produces better outcomes?

What does it take to improve your Interpersonal Skills?

Interpersonal skills require wisdom. It is the wisdom to know how to speak, act, behave, and respond to other people. And wisdom simply means a body of principles that govern the way we act, speak, behave, and respond to other people.

Wisdom guides our perceptions. It guides our discernment as well because we need to have the ability to discern what we say; it guides what responses are appropriate and what response will produce those outcomes as a result of the interaction. By understanding what wisdom is, you can make the connection between wisdom and interpersonal skills, then you realize that it has nothing to do with being shy or introverted.

Having the wisdom to speak, behave, and respond to other people means that you have a body of principles; you have that knowledge base and therefore you've applied that knowledge base enough times to develop it into a skill . And now you have the confidence of that skill and can put it forward into the real world and therefore gain experience on that application of the skill set — that is wisdom.

Shyness or the state of being introverted are personality-driven and to some extent, they are also preferences. So, improving your interpersonal skills does not depend on those elements. There are four key principles to improve your interpersonal skills.

1. Social competency

Having competency means having proficiency in something — it means you have achieved mastery. So, social competency is mastery of a social situation or mastery of a social network. When it comes to social competency, this is where you master the "skill sets" that are relevant and crucial for optimizing interactions with others. This is what most people talk about when they say "improving your interpersonal skills".

It is the number one component of improving interpersonal skills. These skills include communication, conflict management, negotiation, presentation, and self expression. Those are social competencies and it's just one component of interpersonal skills improvement.

So, when you're reading articles or watching videos about interpersonal skills, this is what most people refer to when they think about "how do I improve my interpersonal skills?" But this is only ¼ of it — mastering these particular skill sets.

If you've been researching and learning about interpersonal skills, and you're serious about mastering these skill sets, one of the most important shifts you have to make is understanding that learning things isn't the same as mastering them. Learning something only means you have a cognitive or intellectual understanding of it. But a mere cognitive understanding is not the end goal — the end goal is mastery. When you have mastered something, you no longer need to utilize a lot of your mental resources or effort to perform that skill. Rather it becomes effortless.

Taking communication skills for example; the ability to effectively present your ideas to a non-specialist audience; your ability to persuade your team, bosses, or team supervisors. Achieving mastery in communication means that you can perform those activities without a whole lot of your mental resources.

2. Standards of conscience

This is when you have a standard of how you treat other people, for example. It is also having a moral compass, an inner voice, or a guide that shows us how to behave. It is a moral compass that helps us to have an acute level of awareness of the receptivity of our current behaviors and future behaviors, including our thoughts towards others. One may say that this constitutes outward and inward behavior, respectively.

This is a standard that you have. 'We don't rise to our dreams, we rise to our highest standards.' So your standard of conscience will formulate and guide your philosophy on how you relate with other people. Your standards will also influence how you're able to implement the first principle of social competency.

Although a lot of people understand that we need to have a social conscience, in particular events or situations we still don't know how to act or respond to someone in that moment. It requires a lot of external guidance to help us to hone that skill set. When you master the principle of standard conscience, in any situation you come across in your workforce or in your relationships, or in your life, you'll have the confidence and the courage in how to act.

So, you can see how one principle builds upon the other. While we understand intellectually that it is wise to behave morally, that it is respectable to treat others in a certain way, sometimes there are grey zones. Not everything in a social relationship is black and white. There are these grey zones and these grey zones usually happen in the workplace, especially if you're working in a multicultural organization or in an organization where there are both in-person and online interactions.

Having the standard of conscience and developing mastery around it will help you improve your interpersonal skills.

3. Situational consciousness

This is when you are truly, genuinely, and acutely aware of your surroundings — it means you have situational awareness. Oftentimes, when we are so focused on that one thing we don't see everything around us; the contextual features of it. So, having a situational consciousness means that you're aware of yourself and how you relate to the context around you. It also means that you're aware of the big picture of the situation around you.

This will help guide your actions and also your ability to form mental models of what to do and what to say in those particular situations. Let's face it, any situation you can come across in life has a lot of dynamism; it could be a lot of moving pieces. There could be many things in that environment or event that you don't see and so it requires honing that consciousness.

When you have true awareness around you, sometimes you may realize that your actions or choice or what to do isn't quite the best one moving forward. That's when you realize that there's this part of it that you didn't see before and it's going to change your strategy moving forward so that you can create a sustainable fair exchange in your relationships. And that's how powerful awareness can be.

When it comes to having situational awareness, one of the things that is preventing people from having that acuteness in awareness is that we don't know how to train our brains to filter out what is important. Inside of our brain is a filter system called the reticular activating system. It is a built-in filter right around the back of our brain within the brain stem. This is what helps us to filter what is truly important.

However, our filter is typically filtering based on what we value and what we want to focus on and it is also distracted by our emotions. The key will be in how you hone your situational awareness so that your brain can automatically filter out what is truly important to you so that it'll give you a heightened awareness for you to begin to see things that you would not normally see.

Those who are successful in their career, business, and life tend to be able to see the big picture and interconnectedness of things and then formulate a strategy to get there. They have an acute situational awareness. They have awareness of themselves as they move through an environment as well as the elements of that environment. And they are not overwhelmed by it because they've trained themselves to master developing mental models on how to think about these things.

Again, this requires external guidance to help you to hone that skill set. So that once you develop that skill set with a coach and a mentor you can master the inner guidance, and it'll become an automatic response.

4. Self-Control

This is all about managing your emotions because emotions can be a very strong distractor from our highest values, objectives, and meaningful goals. Even if a lot of people won't admit it, we mostly do things just because we feel like it. When you don't feel like doing something even though you know it's important at that moment, it then becomes the most difficult thing to do. Self-control is about how you influence yourself and how you manage your emotions.

Self-control merges with intrapersonal skills. Although this article is about interpersonal skills, self-control encompasses intrapersonal skills — "intrapersonal" meaning "within the person". The essence of self-control is how you manage yourself. It's all within you. And this falls inside of developing interpersonal skills as well.

Chapter 22

What are Intrapersonal Skills and why are they important?

Intrapersonal skills relate to the self-awareness of our strengths and weaknesses. Intrapersonal skills are a form of self-communication because it relates to what happens within one's inner self.

Intrapersonal skills are what help you manage emotions and cope with challenges you may face at different times in your life. Similar to emotional intelligence, intrapersonal skills include:

- Self-confidence
- Persistence
- Being open to change and new ideas
- Ability to overcome distractions
- Time management
- Resilience
- Self-discipline

Difference between Intrapersonal and Interpersonal Skills

As mentioned, the term 'interpersonal skills' is more commonly known compared to 'intrapersonal skills'. It refers to communication that happens between two or more people, while 'intrapersonal' refers to communication that occurs in your mind. Interpersonal skills can be a verbal or non-verbal exchange of ideas. For many people, interpersonal communication relieves stress, while intrapersonal communication can lead to stress.

Why we need Intrapersonal Skills?

Intrapersonal skills help us achieve as much as possible in life. Knowing what our strengths are and working on our weaknesses can help us perform at work and in our personal lives. Good intrapersonal skills also help build and maintain both personal and working relationships with others, as we're able to manage our emotions, cope with challenges and learn from our experiences.

Strong intrapersonal skills help us focus, set and achieve our goals. People who don't set goals often have nothing to focus on, so they don't achieve as much as someone who has a target to aim for.

For some people, a high level of intrapersonal skills comes naturally, while for others it doesn't. However, it's possible to work on intrapersonal skills to improve them.

How to improve your Intrapersonal Skills?

If you think your intrapersonal skills aren't as sharp as they could be, there are plenty of activities you can do to improve them.

Start a journal

Keeping a journal allows you to track your emotions, goals and daily experiences. Jot down your thoughts and feelings on a daily basis and the journal will be a record of your growth.

Be kind to yourself

Our internal voice is usually the loudest and most critical. Rather than criticising yourself and hoping it will help motivate you, try reminding yourself of your successes and praising yourself for your strengths and achievements. Berating yourself for your short-comings rarely helps.

Set yourself goals

Having short and long term goals gives you something to work towards. Start small with goals that don't overstretch you. Once you have a few wins under your belt, you can expand the goals to something more ambitious. If you don't achieve your goal the first time, don't give up - keep trying. You're building self discipline as you work towards your goals.

Build a healthy habit

In order to achieve your goals, you often need to develop a healthy habit. Taking a little action every day is what helps people achieve their goals. If you build a healthy habit, your goals will be achievable. Remember, it takes about 60 days to develop a habit so aim to stick with it for at least two months. Once you've formed one habit, you can concentrate on a new habit.

Improve your time management skills

To achieve goals and enjoy healthy habits, it helps to have good time management skills. If you recognise that you're easily distracted and you waste large parts of your day, work on improving your time management skills. Prioritise your tasks and then schedule when you'll do each task. Set a timer and work diligently before taking a break and repeating the process. Organise your spaces so you know where everything is, both at work and home, when you need it. Learn to say no if you take on too much so you can work on the things that matter most. Decide when you're most productive and do the important work during these times of the day.

Intrapersonal skills in the workplace

Employees with strong intrapersonal skills are more likely to achieve more than those with poor intrapersonal skills. They can usually cope better in stressful situations, have stronger time management skills so they can juggle conflicting priorities and are more confident in their abilities. When employers assist employees with improving their intrapersonal skills, everyone benefits.

Chapter 23

Achieving happiness through Self-Discipline

Self-discipline and happiness seem to be two contradicting concepts, and using them in the same sentence is unacceptable. Self-discipline brings to mind the idea of "work and effort", while happiness is usually associated with "pleasure" and the absence work.

For most, self-discipline can never be the source of what makes them happy because the relationship with what it means to be happy is misplaced.

Happiness is not the absence of work, it is the absence of guilt, shame, regret, anger, resentment, frustration, sadness, self-doubt, fear, boredom, stress, anxiety, loneliness, and all negative emotions.

Absence of work may give you momentary gratification, but the absence of self-discipline and wasting time with momentary gratifications ultimately results in un-ending negative feelings.

Importance of Self-Discipline

It is an established fact that without discipline, success becomes merely an untranslatable dream. Self-discipline allows you to develop problem solving skills, and helps you make the right choices. It also helps you cultivate strong relationships, and gives you the ability to manage debts, make use of opportunities, and develop a positive attitude towards your health.

This ability to make the right choices at the right time leads to a successful personal and professional life. No one can negate the fact that being blessed in your personal life and having success in your professional life guarantees a certain level of happiness.

Another aspect of being disciplined and happy at the same time is that self-control can help you avoid indulging in problematic situations, distractions and poor habits. This can help you avoid making rash decisions that can cause regret, discontentment, stress, and resentments.

As a disciplined person you are more likely to achieve what you want from life. Victory in life brings confidence and ultimately enables you to embrace the fact that you can achieve anything you want. Furthermore you become proud by the fact that you have achieved success through your own efforts.

A high disposition towards self-discipline enables people to experience fewer problematic desires, and set goals in favor of more virtuous outcomes, which in turn result in a happier life.

How to become Self-Disciplined?

The most tested and proven way to become self-disciplined is to remove distractions and temptations from your environment. If you want to eat healthy, unsubscribe from those fast-food promotional texts you get at lunch from the visiting food truck.

If you want to focus on your project, turn off your cell phone or at least turn off the notifications when it's time to get things done. Keeping your work desk clean and your files organized will also go a long away to help you become more focused. The fewer distractions you face the easier it becomes to stay focused on your goals and tasks.

The other step towards becoming more self-disciplined, is to have set goals and a clear plan to achieve them. By having an action plan that guides you daily towards your goals, you will never get side-tracked. A clear plan that outlines each step towards your goal, will help you stay focused. You can also keep a journal to keep tabs on your plans and use it as a way to check in with yourself on an ongoing basis.

Will-power plays an important role in developing self-discipline. Will-power is elastic and can be stretched to infinity. You can train yourself to control your actions, rather than being on autopilot.

Improving your self-discipline means changing your not so great habits, which at first can be uncomfortable and feel awkward.

Changing habits takes time. Neuroscience says that it usually requires 90 days of repetitive brain-hacking of your beliefs. This is why mantras work so well as a way to re-program your mind to become more disciplined.

Constantly self-regulating, according to morals, standards, and social expectations can result in living a dull, mundane, and joyless life.

The fact is, self-disciplined people start feeling joy in doing things because they create a controlled environment. They are less driven by the need for immediate gratification, or pleasure. They have trained their minds to associate pleasure with the journey life offers.

Contrary to what most believe, disciplined people are not self-denying or unhappy, rather they are happier than many because they have mastered restricting impulses, and temporary pleasures. They have picked virtue over vice.

Self-discipline is about choosing virtues that deliver sustainable joy in your life, and embracing the journey as the adventure instead of the distractions.

Chapter 24

Why Self-Discipline is so hard?

Self-discipline is the ability to control your actions through inner willpower regardless of your emotions and impulses. It's the skill to overcome the temptation to violate your inner principles. Self-discipline enables you to pursue your goals, follow your own ethics, and be the person you want to be. Someone guided by self-discipline uses their mind to make important decisions and aren't led away with the wrong decisions by their feelings.

Why do I struggle with Self-Discipline?

Any struggles you have with self-discipline are normal as people will tend to follow the easiest path of least resistance in life. People will tend to do what feels good in the present moment which makes it difficult to discipline yourself to do what's hard or better for you in the long-term.

A normal person's default setting is instead of doing the hard work, laziness is chosen because it's easy. Uncomfortable work projects are avoided and easier tasks are preferred. People prefer to spend money on small things they want now than to save money for big things they may want later. Debt is preferred over saving and investing. A lack of discipline to do the hard things in life now, many times leads to a much harder life later on.

You struggle with self-discipline because your future goals are not exciting enough to motivate the current you to control your present impulses. If you want more self-discipline you need big exciting goals you are striving toward. The future prize needs to be greater than the current desire.

Is being Disciplined hard?

Being disciplined isn't difficult if you change your beliefs about yourself, your habits, and what you want in life. Staying self-disciplined is much easier when you create systems in your life to build consistent habits. The way you structure your life, the environments you find yourself in, and the temptations you are subjected to have a lot to do with how hard it is for you to maintain your discipline. It's easier to simply avoid temptations and situations altogether than to rely on self-discipline alone.

Discipline is about your present self choosing what's best for your future self. This was found to be much easier if you can relate to your future self. Having empathy for your future selves can help you make better decisions in the present moment.

Does Self-Discipline get easier?

Self-discipline can become easier when you have either positive reinforcement from your future goals or negative reinforcement through future risks. Self-discipline becomes easier if you manage your thoughts carefully and quickly dismiss thoughts encouraging undisciplined actions. It's important to guard your thoughts carefully and only dwell on those that are constructive and positive and leading you toward your bigger goals in life.

Your self-beliefs can also help with your self-discipline. What you believe about yourself can help change your behaviors on both a conscious and subconscious level. If you believe you're a healthy eater then it can become your default setting to choose more nutritious foods. A lot of actions are just reflections of what you believe to be true about yourself. Be careful about what kind of person you believe yourself to be as your actions can reflect this in your behaviors. People seek a confluence between their actions and their belief systems so focus on the positive for more discipline.

Best habits for improving Self-Discipline

Self-discipline is a skill more than a talent. It can be learned through mental focus and practice. Each time you choose to do the right thing you reinforce the skill of discipline. You can create processes in action and thought that help you overcome the temptations of wrong action in real time.

Self-discipline is also like a muscle that must be developed and exercised to grow in strength. The more practice you have in working on and developing your discipline in real-life events, the stronger your will to use it grows. Just like with building real muscles up in size, you must start with smaller mental weights, temptations, and situations to exercise your discipline.

If want to improve your diet you can start with changing one meal at a time each week until you have created a new routine and overcame the smaller temptations of overeating at that one meal before adding a second one. Small successes with discipline build up your confidence and how you see yourself. This helps with the will to keep making the right decisions. Self-discipline is never complete and new challenges will continue to arise but you can be prepared with smaller early victories.

Good stress management is another skill that helps with self-discipline. People have more trouble staying disciplined if they are under great stress that they can't manage or when exhausted. Too many people make impulsive purchases or break their healthy eating habits under stress looking for a relief for how they feel. Incorporating other stress management strategies like meditation or exercise can both be their own practices while also managing stress as a side benefit.

The core of having self-discipline is choosing right action and right thought when you come to a fork in the road on a decision tree. This is where you must make the decision in real time to either go in the direction of your goals and dreams or take a detour back to the road most travelled of hedonism, selfishness, and mediocrity.

Self-discipline can pay very high returns on right effort that is exercised consistently over long periods of time on the correct things. Discipline is the skill of choosing what your best self wants to do in real time regardless of the impulses and desires of your lesser self.

Self-discipline is the core requirement for big success in any area of life, professional or personal.

Chapter 25

Self-Control and Internet Addiction

The Internet has become an indispensable part in a person's daily life, which has brought us both positive and negative effects. One of the typical negative phenomena concerning excessive use of the Internet is Internet addiction. A meta-analysis has found that an estimated 6% of adolescents worldwide have suffered from Internet addiction **(Cheng and Li, 2014)**. It is an impulse-control disorder that does not involve an intoxicant **(Young, 1998a, 2004)**, which has been characterized by poorly-controlled preoccupations, urges, or behaviors regarding Internet access that lead to impairment or distress **(Shaw and Black, 2008)**. Some studies have indicated that Internet addiction disrupts adolescents' time management, especially daily sleep and exercise routines, which weakens their immune system **(Rosen et al., 2014)**, interferes with their social relationships **(Tsitsika et al., 2014)**, hinders academic achievement **(Chou et al., 2005)**, and increases their likelihood of depression symptoms **(Lam and Peng, 2010)**.

Self-control is defined as an inhibition capacity to regulate one's thoughts, emotions, and behaviors in the face of external demands **(DeLisi, 2014)**.

Self-Control and Internet Addiction

We shall first discuss why self-control might be linked to Internet addiction. Then, we will consider how culture, age, gender, Internet addiction measures or publication year might moderate such links.

Restraint, Impulsivity and Internet Addiction

According to impulsiveness theory **(Ainslie, 1975)**, some students have more restraint than others and are less impulsive **(Peluso et al., 1999)**, so they are more likely to sacrifice short-term amusement to invest effort toward attaining long-term goals. For example, students with less restraint than others are more likely to avoid studying for the next day's test by watching videos on the Internet. (Not all uses of the internet are harmful; for example, a student can search for relevant information on the Internet for an essay comparing theocracy in Iran and monarchy in North Korea). By contrast, students with less restraint than others are more likely to make decisions based primarily on short-term benefits (such as watching an Internet video) rather than on investments for long-term benefits, like studying for a test **(Metcalfe and Mischel, 1999; Duckworth and Steinberg, 2015)**. If such students with less restraint have few other means to satisfy their emotional needs, they might increasingly use the Internet to do so **(Ponton and Rhea, 2006)**. Thus, their repeated decisions to enjoy Internet use can foster Internet addiction **(Baumeister et al., 2010; Shek and Lu, 2012)**. In contrast, other researchers argue that such decisions need not be impulsive, so that self-control might be unrelated to Internet addiction **(e.g., Hur, 2006)**. In other words, when students are addicted to the Internet, they make rational decisions because they know the characteristics of the Internet as anonymity, convenience, and escape, not because of impulse **(Young, 1998a)**.

Past studies of self-control and Internet addiction have shown mixed results. Some studies have revealed that restraint indicators (e.g., impulse control and resist temptation) are negatively related to Internet addiction **(Larose et al., 2003; Kim et al., 2008; Li et al., 2014)**. Also, other studies have demonstrated that impulsivity indicators (e.g., impulsivity and temper) are positively related to Internet addiction **(Gao and Zhao, 2009; Tao and Li, 2009)**.

However, many other studies have shown no significant relationship. Some studies have found no significant link between restraint indicators (e.g., self-control, self-regulation, etc.) and Internet addiction **(Iftikhar**

and Tariq, 2014; Lee and Cho, 2015; Błachnio and Przepiorka, 2016). Likewise, other studies have shown no significant link between impulsivity indicators (e.g., impulsivity, dyscontrol, etc.) and Internet addiction **(Choi et al., 2013; Öğütçü et al., 2016; Zhou, 2017).** Although moderators (e.g., culture, age, and gender) might account for some of these differences in results, most studies did not test for them **(Teng et al., 2014)**. Also, some of these differences in results might stem from using different measures (restraint vs. impulsivity indicators, different Internet addiction measures) or across the years of the studies. Hence, we consider possible moderation effects in the next section.

Moderation: Culture, Age, Gender, Internet Addiction Measures and Year

As many studies include information on the participants' culture, age, gender, internet addiction measures and year, our meta-analysis can test for their moderation effects. Hence, we discuss the potential moderation of each variable.

Culture

A society's cultural values might moderate the link between self-control and Internet addiction. While some societies highlight short-term goals [e.g., United States (US)], others encourage attention to long-term goals (e.g., China; Hofstede et al., 2008). As emphasis of long-term goals can reinforce their importance to students with restraint, they might attend to and devote effort to these long-term goals **(Dewitte and Cremer, 2001)**, thereby further reducing the attractiveness of short-term Internet amusements and the likelihood of Internet addiction. For example, the correlation between restraint and Internet addiction is weak among university students in the United Kingdom **(Mehroof and Griffiths, 2010)** but much stronger among those in mainland China **(Du, 2013).** However, other studies show strong negative links in the United States **(Khang et al., 2013)** and the Netherlands **(Van Deursen et al., 2015)** but weak negative links in South Korea **(Lee and Cho, 2015).**

In contrast, students with low self-control are likely to ignore such long-term goals, so this cultural value is not likely to influence them **(Metcalfe and Mischel, 1999)**. Hence, the link between impulsivity indicators and Internet addiction is likely substantial across countries. For example, studies show moderate to large links between impulsivity indicators and

Internet addiction in Australia **(Chou and Ting, 2003),** Canada **(Davis et al., 2002)**, mainland China **(Bai and Xu, 2009),** Hungary **(Demetrovics et al., 2016),** and South Korea **(Choi et al., 2014).**

Thus, a society with a long-term orientation might further strengthen the negative link between restraint and Internet addiction. However, this cultural value might not moderate the positive link between impulsivity and Internet addiction. Hence, this meta-analysis tested whether the link between self-control and Internet addiction differed across countries.

Age

Among low self-control students, younger students' impulsivity might render them more vulnerable to Internet addiction **(Wang et al., 2017),** but university students' loss of friendships and parental monitoring might increase their loneliness and likelihood of seeking solace on the Internet **(Throuvala et al., 2019; Teng et al., 2020)**. On the one hand, as children grow into adults, their brains develop; specifically, their anterior insulas become thinner **(Churchwell and Yurgelun-Todd, 2013)**, so they become less impulsive and plan more (**Steinberg et al., 2008; Kasen et al., 2011)**. As a result, less impulsive, older students might be less susceptible to short-term Internet amusements and hence less likely to suffer from Internet addiction.

On the other hand, university students often move into a new environment without their family and old friends **(Asendorpf, 2002).** So, university students might feel lonelier and have less parent monitoring than otherwise, both of which might encourage impulsive university students to engage in more Internet activity and subsequently suffer from Internet addiction **(Bozoglan et al., 2013; Yao et al., 2014)**. When students move away to university, they generally have fewer opportunities to keep their parents and childhood friends company, and making new friends might require substantial effort **(Mattanah et al., 2010)**. As a result, they often miss their family (homesickness) and friends (friendsickness, Paul and Brier, 2001) and feel lonely **(Larose and Boivin, 1998)**. Such lonely university students with impulsivity are easily tempted by the ready availability and immediate gratification of Internet entertainment. Without their parents or other family members nearby to monitor them **(Henderson and Mapp, 2002),** such impulsive university students might spend excessive time on the Internet and become addicted.

In summary, the research literature suggests two conflicting hypotheses. On the one hand, younger children are more impulsive than older children, more inclined to indulge in immediate Internet enjoyment excessively, and thus more likely to become addicted. On the other hand, older university students might feel lonely, use the Internet excessively without parent monitoring, and become addicted. As students with restraint are more disciplined and more focused on long-term goals, they are likely less susceptible to short-term amusements and Internet addiction. As few studies examined students at different ages, this meta-analysis can help determine whether age moderates the link between self-control and Internet addiction.

Gender

Unlike males, females pay more attention to their peers, monitor one another's actions more, and are more influenced by one another **(Rudman and Goodwin, 2004; Wills et al., 2004).** In contrast, males are less attentive to their peers and less influenced by them, relying more on their judgments **(Charness and Rustichini, 2011)**. As many males rely more on themselves than on their peers compared with females, males' self-control is more likely to affect their behaviors and outcomes **(Benda, 2013; Koon–Magnin et al., 2016),** such as Internet addiction. Hence, we expect the link between self-control and Internet addiction to be stronger for males than for females.

Internet Addiction Measures and Year

In this study, we examine whether the following three Internet addiction measures moderate findings regarding the relationship between self-control and Internet addiction. Most past studies collected data on Internet addiction via surveys. For example, Young's (1998b) **Internet Addiction Test (IAT)** comprises 20 items with a five-point scoring system, in which normal Internet users typically have a total score below 50 points. Higher total scores indicate greater severity of Internet addiction. Caplan's (2002) **Generalized Problematic Internet Use Scale (GPIUS)** consists of 29 items with a five-point scoring system, capturing mood alteration, social benefits, negative outcomes, compulsivity, excessive time, withdrawal, and interpersonal control. Chen et al.'s (2003) **Chinese Internet Addiction Scale (CIAS)** has 26 items with a four-point scale and focuses on five constructs: compulsive use, withdrawal, tolerance, interpersonal relationship difficulties and health/time management difficulties. Other

Internet addiction scales [e.g., Brenner's (1997) **Internet-Related Addictive Behavior Inventory (IRABI)]** have not been widely used to study self-control and Internet addiction.

The internet has substantially changed over time, especially the increase in social media activities (Leung, 2014). Hence, we also test for differences across years.

Purpose of this study

This study aims to (a) synthesize the results of past studies on the relation between self-control and Internet addiction among students (10–22 years old) and (b) identify factors that influence this relationship. Specifically, this meta-analysis (a) calculates the overall effect size of the link between self-control and Internet addiction and (b) determines whether culture, age, gender, Internet addiction measures or publication year moderated this link.

Conclusion

The meaning of 'Self-Discipline' can be simplified as having self control. Self-Discipline can be defined as a orderly function of controlling one's feelings and dealing with all odds maturely ensuring complete positivity and total control.

Everyone has goals and desires to achieve in their life, we all want the best of everything around us. Be it money, health, family or professional success, everybody wants it. But the truth is that not everyone is able to achieve the desired results.

What is that one thing which makes only few people to achieve their dreams and goals while others don't reach even closer to it?

Self-discipline to achieve something is an extremely important step after deciding on to your goal and working out the plan of action. To act on to something one requires an extensive amount of self discipline. This is one thing which makes achievers a step ahead than those who fail in their lives.

To many, self-discipline sounds as a tedious task but if taken small steps towards it, great benefits will be reaped out of it.

1. Take small steps

Nothing can be achieved in a fortnight, not even self discipline. One needs to take smaller steps towards it, starting from a very small task to begin with. For example, if you are trying to lose weight and are not able to work on your diet regime, it is good to start by controlling the diet with a small step.

Like you can decide to eat chocolate once or twice a week rather than giving up completely. Once you are able to achieve it, this will develop a confidence to work towards it further.

2. Find out your motivation

To be self-discipline motivation is required. Motivation comes from a purpose, find out the main reason for your goal intended to achieve. For example, you are looking towards a promotion so you want to give that extra effort in your work. Or you want to lose some weight to be physically fit or to fit in a certain dress.

Every time your mind tries to skip the path of self discipline; this motivating factor will bring you back on track to achieve it.

3. Create the right environment

To achieve self-discipline, it is important to have a right kind of surrounding since it will help not to deviate from the path itself. For example, if you plan to get up early, then it is important to sleep early in night, this will happen by not watching late night TV and having early dinner.

If you know resisting junk food is hard for you, in the process of losing weight then prevent keeping any of it in your home or workspace.

4. Know the right way of self-discipline

Self=discipline should be implemented in the right way. First of all know your goal that you want to achieve, then figure out the correct plan of action to be implemented towards it. It does not make sense that a person is not eating right and complains of not losing weight despite of exercising.

It is essential to understand that to achieve a desired goal required commitment in all forms. As much exercising is important, taking care of a good diet is also required to lose weight and be fit.

5. Get into sports or in an art form

Sports are the best way to develop self-discipline. The rules of a certain sports not only helps to understand the discipline but regular practice also helps to motivate to develop self discipline which can be implemented in other areas of life.

Also playing instrument, painting, crafts or dance, any of these forms helps to build the self-discipline. Since these are fun to do therefore it is easier to build the discipline required.

6. Find your inspiration

Read autobiography of any famous personality. Every successful individual will talk about the importance of self discipline in their life. To be successful in life is no magic, if one can do it then anyone can do it. Also, talk to the people around you whom you consider successful, understand what made them achieve their goals and how did they maintain the self discipline.

7. Learn to say 'no' to self

Temptations are a major concern initially when one is trying to achieve self discipline. One needs to understand that it is just a temporary phase and if these temptations are fought back they will not come again. Say no to yourself when you want to have that extra piece of cake or feel like sleeping for five more minutes.

If one is stuck and agrees to these temptations then the cause of achievement will be lost. Therefore, getting ahead past of these will help in beneficial results.

8. Make it fun

Most of the people fail to achieve self discipline because they see it as a task to be done, making it sound more tedious than it could. Let it be a fun event or a moment to enjoy. For example, if gym is something hard to keep up with, then join a dance class or yoga whichever suits you.

Play music while exercising or imagine getting a chance to see and experience the sunrise if you get up early in the morning. The more it is fun; the easier it is to follow.

9. Repetition is important

It is easier to slip from the path of discipline. Lot of people think that they have achieved what it requires to be disciplined, but it is important to understand that self discipline is to be implemented daily. In case if you slip in between, it is best to pick up from where you left and start moving forward.

10. Fix a time

Understand the best suitable time to do something. For exercising, see if it is convenient to work out in the morning or evenings. A good time makes it easier to enact on it hence reduces the chance of failure.

If you intend to start reading a book then it is good to see which part of the day you are attentive to read a book, there is no point if you are drowsing and trying to read a book.

11. Visualize the benefits

The best way to keep up with the self discipline is to know what the benefits one will be getting in future are. See what exactly you want it to be and how it should be.

The happiness getting from the process of visualization will help in working towards your goal and hence creating the required self discipline.

12. Be ready to pay the price for the benefits

As per a survey, the most successful people in the world tend to sleep only four hours a day. Those extra hours out of bed makes them work a bit more than others and let them step ahead than others. These successful people are same as all of us and at times they would love to sleep a bit more every morning.

But they let their motivations and goals get ahead than the tiny lazy voice in the head. This requires an immense amount of self discipline. If one is able to conquer the tiny voice in head then being successful is not a distant dream.

13. Be a part of a group

Sometimes it is difficult to achieve self discipline on our own, therefore, it is good to take a help from a friend or meet people with similar goals. Motivating and keep a check on each other helps a lot.

For example, if you have a hard time exercising all by yourself then take help from a friend who is also in need to work out. Both of them keep a check on the other and ensure that the other one is not deviating from the path.

14. Have a goal

Many a times people are not self-disciplined as they do not have a goal or a cause to be disciplined. Having a goal and ambition in life creates a path to be walked on, when a path is there then the idea how to travel comes along which leads to create a space for self-discipline. Having a goal in life will definitely bring positive changes in life.

Self-discipline is the required instrument to achieve benefits and goals in life. Initially, it might seem as a task unachievable but with time it will benefit the individual.

It is to be noted, that the benefits reaped for long terms are a lot better than the short term benefits of avoiding self-discipline. So get the best out of everything and bring some change in your life.

*****

www.ingramcontent.com/pod-product-compliance
Ingram Content Group UK Ltd.
Pitfield, Milton Keynes, MK11 3LW, UK
UKHW042014190726
13854UKWH00005B/2287

9 789358 059090